'ULŪM AL-QUR'ĀN

An Introduction to the Sciences of the Qur'ān

AHMAD VON DENFFER

The Islamic Foundation

ISBN 0 86037 248 0 (Paperback)

Published by
The Islamic Foundation
Markfield Dawah Centre,
Ratby Lane,
Markfield,
Leicester LE67 9RN,
United Kingdom

Quran House,
PO Box 30611,
Nairobi,
Kenya

PMB 3193,
Kano,
Nigeria

British Library Cataloguing in Publication Data
Denffer, Ahmad von
'Ulūm al-Qur'ān: an introduction to the sciences of the Qur'ān
1. Koran – Commentaries
I. Title
297'.1226 BP130.4

Printed in Great Britain by The Cromwell Press, Melksham, Wiltshire

بسم الله الرحمن الرحيم

Contents

In the Name of Allah, the Merciful, the Mercy-giving.

Preface

The Qur'ān, while being revealed, was a living event for those who heard it. It was a part of their lives; rather the *life* itself, and not merely a book. One hardly needs a whole lot of external aids to understand one's own life. However, the words that were alive were also being written down; becoming the Book. Some loss is inevitable in such a process – the text no more remains *as* alive, as understandable, for all the subsequent hearers as for the first – yet there is no alternative to it. For without having been written down, the priceless treasure could not have been transferred from one generation to another. But a written text, over time, stands in need of more and more external aids to make itself clear. It was therefore natural and inevitable that various branches of knowledge centred around the Qur'ān should have arisen to help in understanding it.

It was in the lifetime of the Prophet himself, blessings and peace be upon him, that the development of disciplines and branches of knowledge which were related to the understanding of the Qur'ān and considered necessary for this purpose – what we call the *'ulūm al-qur'ān* – began. The need to understand what the various words and texts correctly and fully meant was present from the very beginning; thus the rudiments of exegesis *(tafsīr)* and lexicon *(mufradāt, gharā'ib, lugha)* were laid. Gradually the range of questions became wider and wider. What was revealed when and where? On what occasion and under what circumstances? Were variant readings permissible; and, if permissible, what were those? Which verses superseded which? How was the Qur'ān arranged and how was it gathered? These are only some of the questions which were raised and answered. Around these answers developed the *'ulūm al-qur'ān*.

Writing books was the hallmark of Islamic culture; the *'ulūm al-qur'ān* were no exception. Books on various aspects began to be compiled in the very first century of Hijra: for example, the first books on *tafsīr* are attributed to the Companions, Ubay Ibn Ka'b and 'Abdullāh Ibn 'Abbās, and to Sa'īd Ibn Jubair (d. 93H); 'Ikrima (d. 107H) wrote on the reasons and circumstances of revelation. By the end of the third century, a very large number of books appear to have been written, but none of them were comprehensive and all of them are not extant. The need of a systematic, comprehensive compilation must have been felt. The first such work is reported to have been written by Abū Bakr Muḥammad Ibn Khalaf (d. 309H) in 27 volumes, known as *al-ḥādī fī 'ulūm al-qur'ān,* but the first extant book is that of Burhānuddīn Zarkashī (d. 794H), *al-burhān fī 'ulūm al-qur'ān.* This was followed by Jalāluddīn Suyūṭī's (d. 911H) *al-itqān fī 'ulūm al-qur'ān,* based mostly on Zarkashī's *al-burhān.* Suyūṭī's *al-itqān* serves as a standard source book on the *'ulūm al-qur'ān.*

However, there was no book in English language on this subject. Brother Ahmad von Denffer has therefore rendered a great service by compiling the first English book, which fills a very serious and deeply-felt gap. An average English reader, especially a student, who has no access to an Arabic text like *al-itqān,* had nothing to help him in understanding the Qur'ān. Ahmad's book should now provide valuable assistance to him in his task.

I believe that one can still absorb the message of the Qur'ān without any external aid, if one goes to it in an appropriate way. But to understand the meaning of all the verses without a knowledge of the *'ulūm al-qur'ān* would be well nigh impossible. Hence the information provided by Ahmad von Denffer should prove indispensible to anyone who cannot reach the Arabic sources. It is precise, brief, yet quite comprehensive.

I am happy that the Islamic Foundation is publishing such a useful work. I pray to Allah *subḥānahū wa ta'ālā* to accept our humble efforts and to grant us His mercy and forgiveness.

Dhū al-Qa'da 1403
August 1983
Leicester, U.K.

Khurram Murad
Director General

Foreword to the Second Edition

This book, an introduction to the Sciences of the Qur'ān, was compiled more than a decade ago and since then it has run into two reprint editions. For some time it has been out of print. The book has received acclamation from many quarters and there was a need to bring out a revised edition, eliminating some of the printing mistakes and standardizing the system of transliteration.

In this new edition, therefore, we have tried to correct such mistakes, standardize the transliteration of Arabic and foreign words and have made a few necessary minor additions. Modern researches have been duly credited in a supplementary bibliography. I hope readers of *'Ulūm al-Qur'ān* will find the book of great value and will benefit immensely from the new bibliographical information.

I am grateful to my colleagues, in particular Mokrane Guezzou, for going through the book and suggesting necessary alterations and corrections. May Allah accept this humble contribution of the Foundation and make it a source of reference for students of the Qur'ān.

Rabīʿ al-Awwal 1415
August 1994

M. Manazir Ahsan
Director General

Introduction

The Qur'ān contains the revelations of Allah, the Creator and Sustainer of the Universe, to mankind. It is the message from God to man and therefore of utmost importance to us. To properly grasp a message, one needs first of all to understand its contents exactly, and for this purpose one must study the Qur'ān deeply and in detail. In fact, some people do spend their whole lives studying the Qur'ān, reading and reflecting upon it and, as they grow and develop, both physically and spiritually, they discover for themselves new meanings and implications.

Secondly, some special knowledge of the circumstances that surround the message is also necessary for fuller understanding of its meaning and implications. Although some part of this special knowledge can be derived from the Qur'ān itself, there remain other areas of knowledge that can only be discovered by wider study and research.

Muslims have from earliest times, applied themselves not only to the message from Allah – the Qur'ān – but also to its setting and framework, and the preoccupation with these ultimately developed into the 'sciences' of or 'knowledge' about the Qur'ān, known as '*'ulūm al-qur'ān*'.

The proper approach to the Qur'ān, in my humble view, can be described in three stages. You must:

first, *receive* the message of the Qur'ān, by hearing or reading it;

second, *understand* the message of the Qur'ān by reflecting upon it and studying its meanings;

third, *apply* the message of the Qur'ān by ordering your personal life as well as the life of society according to its message.

The branch of knowledge, called *'ulūm al-qur'ān* may be used as a means for the accomplishment of the second stage, understanding the message of the Qur'ān, by understanding its setting and circumstances.

According to a general definition, *'ulūm al-qur'ān*[1] denotes studies concerned with the book of revelations sent down upon the last Prophet Muḥammad,[2] namely:

— Its revelation.
— Its collection.
— Its order and arrangement.
— Its writing down.
— Information about the reasons and occasions of revelation.
— About what was revealed in Makka and what in Madina.
— About the abrogating and abrogated verses.
— About the 'clear' and the 'unclear' verses.

The term also covers Qur'ān-related studies, such as:

— The explanation of verses and passages by the Prophet himself, his Companions, their followers and the later exegetes of the Qur'ān.
— The methods of explanation.
— The scholars of exegesis and their books.

The aim of this book – as all *'ulūm al-qur'ān* – is to help towards a better understanding of the Qur'ānic message by providing information on its setting, framework and circumstances. To a great extent it is a descriptive account of the traditional subject of *'ulūm al-qur'ān*. Some branches of *'ulūm al-qur'ān*, such as the divisions of the text, style, literary form etc., have only been touched upon briefly, while others that seemed more important have been dealt with in more detail. In particular such topics related to the understanding of the text (*asbāb al-nuzūl*, *al-nāsikh wa al-mansūkh*, etc.) have been treated more extensively while others, such as the *'seven aḥruf'* or the *'Uthmānic writing*, which are of benefit only to readers with a good knowledge of classical Arabic, have been introduced, but not elaborated upon.

1 Ṣābūnī, Muḥammad 'Alī: *al-tibyān fī 'ulūm al-qur'ān*, Beirut, 1970, p.10.
2 The customary blessings on the Prophet (Allah's blessings and peace be upon him) each time his name is mentioned will not be repeated in the text, but the reader is kindly requested to observe this Muslim tradition.

I have restricted myself to presenting the generally-accepted views on the issues and, where no consensus exists, have referred to the most important of the divergent opinions. Although I do have my own views on some questions, my basic aim in this 'Introduction' is generally to inform the reader about the subject, and not to guide him – overtly or covertly – towards my own conclusions.

There are a number of matters related to the study of the Qur'ān to which I have drawn special attention since this 'Introduction' to the *'ulūm al-qur'ān* is aimed at a special readership, namely, young educated Muslims with little or no access to the original sources on the subject. I have therefore included several topics, of special relevance for that readership, such as:

— Orientalists and the Qur'ān.
— Translations of the Qur'ān.
— Modern interpretation of the Qur'ān.
— Language of the Qur'ān.
— Reading and recitation of the Qur'ān.

Again, particularly for the benefit of these readers, I have often quoted typical examples to illustrate the various points discussed and make them more easily comprehensible.

Finally, to assist readers not familiar with Arabic, I have supplied references to English translations, where available (such as translation of *ḥadīth* books, etc.). However, on certain topics (e.g. *asbāb al-nuzūl* or *al-nāsikh wa al-mansūkh*) there is no literature available as yet in English and references had to be restricted to Arabic sources only.

I have also attempted to note in the bibliography at least one or two books in English for each section, from which more insight may be gained on the topic discussed.

May this volume (to the best of my knowledge, the first of its kind in a European language) fulfil its purpose and assist you to grasp fully the message of the Qur'ān and to apply it in your life, and may Allah accept this humble effort and forgive its shortcomings.

Leicester
Ramadan 1981/1401

Ahmad von Denffer

CHAPTER 1

The Qur'ān and Revelation

REVELATION AND SCRIPTURE BEFORE THE QUR'ĀN

God's Communication with Man

God communicated with man. This is the key concept of revelation upon which all religious belief – if more than a mere philosophical attempt to explain man's relationship with the great 'unknown', the 'wholly other' – is founded. There is no religious belief, however remote it may be in time or concept from the clear teachings of Islam, which can do without or has attempted to do without God's communication with man.

Man denies God

God's communication with man has always accompanied him, from the earliest period of his appearance on this planet, and throughout the ages until today. Men have often denied the communication from God or attributed it to something other than its true source and origin. More recently some have begun to deny God altogether, or to explain away man's preoccupation with God and the communication from Him as a preoccupation with delusion and fantasy. Yet even such people do not doubt that the preoccupation of man with God's communication is as old as man himself. Their reasoning is, they claim, based on material evidence. Following this line of thought they feel that they should deny God's existence, but are at the same time compelled to concede the point – for material evidence is abundant – that man has ever been preoccupied with thinking about God and the concept of God's communication with man.

Empiricism and Reality

Their general approach – to emphasise material evidence – in the search for reality and truth, is surely commendable. Not only empiricist philosophy but also commonsense tell us that one should accept as real and existent what can be grasped empirically, that is, by direct experience, by seeing, hearing, touching and so on. While there may be in other systems of thought, other criteria for the evaluation of reality, at present it is a materialistic philosophy that rules the day, and though many people (especially the 'religious' type) are saddened by this and wish back the 'old days of idealism and rule of the creed', I personally think that we have to accept the present state of affairs – not as ideal and unchangeable, but as our point of departure – and moreover that doing so is of some advantage to us.

Creation is Material Evidence for God

Many now accept empiricism as their guiding principles and God gives ample evidence, material evidence, capable of verification by all empiricists, for His being and existence. The wide earth, the whole universe of creation, are evidence, material evidence, for God. No empiricist would deny that the earth and the universe do exist. It is only that he does not always perceive them as 'creation', for then he would have to argue from the material evidence that he has to a mighty and puissant cause, to reason and purpose behind it. Such an argument would by no means be in contradiction with his empiricist, rational and scientific line of thought, rather in perfect agreement with it.

Man's Pride

I do not wish to discuss here in any detail why then, despite this, man denies God and disregards His communication with man. Suffice to say that the cause must be seen in man's self-perception, his arrogance and false pride. Having discovered that he and his kind constitute the peak of 'creation', he thinks himself autonomous, self-dependent, absolutely free and fully equipped to be master of the universe. Somehow, this self-perception too has been with man from his early days. He has always thought himself better than anything else.[1]

Guidance for Man

Muslims, referring to the Holy Qur'ān, also conclude that from the beginning of his life on earth, man has received communication from God, to guide him and protect him from such self-perception and deceit:

> 'We said: Get ye down all from here; and if, as is sure, there comes to you guidance from Me, whosoever follows My guidance on them shall be no fear, nor shall they grieve' (2:38).[2]

This message and promise has been communicated by God to all mankind, all children of Adam, as the Qur'ān explains:

> 'O ye children of Adam! Whenever there come to you apostles from amongst you, rehearsing My signs unto you – those who are righteous and mend (their lives) – on them shall be no fear nor shall they grieve' (7:35).

The Messengers

The guidance from God comes through the apostles or

1 The question of *how* evil came into the world has preoccupied many sincere seekers after the truth. The answer which the Qur'ān gives is simple yet convincing if seen against all the evidence of historical and contemporary human civilisation. At the root of all evil in this world is disobedience to God, resulting from the belief that one is superior to another. From this belief stems oppression of man by man, discrimination, crime and all other evils that rule the day. The test lies in obedience to God, for seen against God, the 'wholly other', all creation is indeed on the other side and equal. In *Sūra al-a'rāf* (7) it is related that God asked all angels to bow before Adam, the first man. The angels obeyed, and observed God's will, except Iblīs. When asked why he opposed God's will, he replied: '*anā khairun minhu*' – I (Iblīs) am better than him (Adam), you created me from fire and created him from clay' (7:12). This then is the beginning of all evil, for it is Iblīs who after this makes it his mission to incite men also to act against God's will.

2 I shall use the following two English translations of the Holy Qur'ān: A. Yusuf Ali, (Ali, Abdullah Yusuf: *The Glorious Qur'ān: Text, Translation and Commentary.* Leicester, 1978) and M. Pickthall (Pickthall, Mohammad Marmaduke: *The Meaning of the Glorious Koran*, New York, 1963).

messengers, and they bring with them the scripture from God:

> 'We sent before time Our apostles with clear signs and sent down with them the book and the balance (of right and wrong) that men may stand forth in justice . . .' (57:25).

The basic message of all prophets from God, and hence of all scriptures they brought, is one and the same message from God to man:'

> 'And verily We have raised in every nation a messenger, (proclaiming): Serve Allah and shun false gods . . .' (16:36).

The Names of the Prophets and their Number

The Qur'ān mentions the following prophets by name: Ādam, Nūḥ, Ibrāhīm, Ismā'īl, Isḥāq, Lūṭ, Ya'qūb, Yūsuf, Mūsā, Hārūn, Dāwūd, Sulaimān, Ilyās, Al-Yasa', Yūnus, Ayyūb, Zakarīyā, Yaḥyā, 'Īsā, Idrīs, Hūd, Dhul Kifl, Shu'aib, Ṣāliḥ, Luqmān, Dhul Qarnain, 'Uzair, Muḥammad.

This does not mean, however, that only these have been God's prophets. Indeed the Qur'ān is very clear that the number of prophets is much larger and that to each community from among mankind God has sent His messenger:

> 'We did aforetime send apostles before thee: of them there are some whose story We have related to thee and some whose story We have not related to thee. . .' (40:78).
>
> 'To every people (was sent) an apostle. . .' (10:47).

The Names of the Scriptures and their Number

Just as there have been numerous prophets so there were numerous written records of their messages. The Qur'ān mentions the following revelations in particular, which are sometimes called sheets or leaves (*ṣuḥuf*) and sometimes book or scripture (*kitāb*):

— The ‘sheets’ of Ibrāhīm and Mūsā.
— The Torah (*taurāt*) of Mūsā.
— The Psalms (*zabūr*) of Dāwūd.
— The Gospel (*injīl*) of ‘Īsā.
— The Qur’ān of Muḥammad.

The Contents of the Former Scriptures

All the teachings contained in the former Scriptures that were meant to be of lasting value and importance are included in the Qur’ān. The Qur’ān also gives some specific accounts, although selective, of what the pre-Qur’ānic scriptures contained and it is worthwhile to look briefly at this material:

A reference to the ‘sheets’ (*ṣuḥuf*) of Ibrāhīm and Mūsā:

> ‘But those will prosper who purify themselves, and glorify the name of their guardian Lord, and (lift their hearts) in prayer. Nay, behold, ye prefer the life of this world; but the Hereafter is better and more enduring’ (87: 14-17).[3]

A reference to the Torah (*taurāt*) of Mūsā:

> ‘It was We who revealed the law (to Moses): therein was guidance and light . . .
> We ordained therein for them: life for life, eye for eye, nose for nose, ear for ear, tooth for tooth and wounds equal for equal, but if anyone remits the retaliation by way of charity it is an act of atonement for himself and if any fail to judge by (the light of) what God has revealed they are (no better than) wrongdoers’ (5: 47-8).

A reference to the Psalms (*zabūr*) of Dāwūd:

> ‘And verily We have written in the Psalms, after the

---

3 Some say that the whole of *Sūra* 87 is a reference to this first book of revelation, but others hold that only the few verses quoted here are actually meant. See *mukhtaṣar tafsīr Ibn Kathīr*, Beirut, 1402/1981, Vol. 3, p.631. Another reference to the *ṣuḥuf* of Mūsā and Ibrāhīm is in *Sūra* 53: 36 ff.

Reminder: My righteous slaves will inherit the earth' (21: 105).

A reference to the Gospel (*injīl*) of 'Īsā:

> 'Muḥammad is the messenger of Allah. And those with him are hard against the disbelievers and merciful among themselves. Thou (O Muḥammad) seest them bowing and falling prostrate (in worship) seeking bounty from Allah and (His) acceptance. The mark of them is on their foreheads from the traces of prostration. Such is their likeness in the Torah and their likeness in the Gospel – like as sown corn that sendeth forth its shoot and strengtheneth it and riseth firm upon its stalk, delighting the sowers – that He may enrage the disbelievers with (the sight of) them. Allah has promised, unto such of them as believe and do good works, forgiveness and immense reward' (48: 29).

The pre-Qur'ānic scriptures, besides carrying the same basic message about Allah, the Master of the worlds, and man, His creation, also brought specific instructions addressed directly to particular communities of people at given points of time in history and in particular circumstances, such as the Jewish or Christian communities. Revelation before the Qur'ān, and hence scriptures before it, were in many of their details situation-oriented in nature and therefore confined to their particular frameworks. This also explains the continuity of revelation. With changing circumstances and in different situations new guidance from Allah was required. As long as the revelation and scripture were not completely universal in nature, revelation would not reach its finality.

The Final Revelation

Muḥammad was the last messenger from Allah to mankind, and he brought the final revelation from God to man. Therefore the scripture containing this revelation is the last of the Holy Scriptures.

The basic message of the Holy Qur'ān is the same as the

basic message of the previous revelations and books, and the directives and instructions, by which it provides guidance for man are of a universal nature. They apply for all times to come and in all situations. This revelation corresponds to man's position on earth and in history. Man has reached, in his development, the stage when universal principles need to be applied to safeguard his purposeful existence.

THE QUR'ĀN, ḤADĪTH AND ḤADĪTH QUDSĪ

The Qur'ān

The Qur'ān can be defined as follows:

— The speech of Allah,
sent down upon the last Prophet Muḥammad,
through the Angel Gabriel,
in its precise meaning and precise wording,
transmitted to us by numerous persons (*tawātur*),
both verbally and in writing.

— Inimitable and unique,
protected by God from corruption.

The word Qur'ān

The Arabic word '*qur'ān*' is derived from the root *qara'a*, which has various meanings, such as to read,[4] to recite,[5] etc. *Qur'ān* is a verbal noun and hence means the 'reading' or 'recitation'. As used in the Qur'ān itself, the word refers to the revelation from Allah in the broad sense[6] and is not always restricted to the written form in the shape of a book, as we have it before us today.

However, it means revelation to Muḥammad only, while revelation to other prophets has been referred to by different names (e.g. *taurāt*, *injīl*, *kitāb*, etc.).

---

4 *Sūra* 17:93.
5 *Sūra* 75: 18: 17:46.
6 *Sūra* 17:82.

Other Names of the Qur'ān

The revelation from Allah to the Prophet Muḥammad is referred to – in the Qur'ān itself – by the name *qur'ān* (recitation) as well as by other names, such as e.g.

— *furqān* (criterion, see 25: 1).
— *tanzīl* (sent down, see 26: 192).
— *dhikr* (reminder, see 15: 9).
— *kitāb* (scripture, see 21: 10).

Other references to the Qur'ān are by such words as *nūr* (light), *hudā* (guidance), *raḥma* (mercy), *majīd* (glorious), *mubārak* (blessed), *bashīr* (announcer), *nadhīr* (warner), etc.

All these names reflect one of the various aspects of the revealed word of Allah.

The Meaning of Ḥadīth[7]

The word *ḥadīth* means news, report or narration. It is in this general sense that the word is used in the Qur'ān.[8]

Technically, the word *ḥādīth*, (pl. *aḥādīth*) means in particular the reports (verbal and written) about the *sunna* of the Prophet Muḥammad. *Ḥadīth* reports about the Prophet Muḥammad are of the following kinds:

— What he said (*qaul*).
— What he did (*fi'l*).
— What he (silently) approved (*taqrīr*) in others' actions.

There are also reports about him, i.e. about what he was like (*ṣifa*).

The difference between the Qur'ān and Ḥadīth.

There is agreement among most Muslim scholars that the

7 For details on *ḥadīth* see: A'zami, Muhammad Mustafa: *Studies in Hadith Methodology and Literature*, Indianapolis, 1977.

8 e.g. *Sūra* 12:101.

contents of the *sunna* are also from Allah. Hence they have described it as also being the result of some form of inspiration.[9] The contents of the *sunna* are however expressed through the Prophet's own words or actions, while in the case of the Qur'ān the Angel Gabriel brought the exact wording and contents to the Prophet, who received this as revelation and then announced it, in the very same manner that he received it.

The difference between these two forms has been illustrated by Suyūṭī (following Juwainī) in the following manner:

> 'The revealed speech of Allah is of two kinds: As to the first kind, Allah says to Gabriel: Tell the Prophet to whom I sent you that Allah tells him to do this and this, and He ordered him something. So Gabriel understood what His Lord had told him. Then he descended with this to the Prophet and told him what His Lord had told him, but the expression is not this (same) expression, just as a king says to someone upon whom he relies: Tell so-and-so: The king says to you: strive in his service and gather your army for fighting . . . and when the messenger (goes and) says: The king tells you: do not fail in my service, and do not let the army break up, and call for fighting, etc., then he has not lied nor shortened (the message) . . .
>
> 'And as to the other kind, Allah says to Gabriel: Read to the Prophet this (piece of) writing, and Gabriel descended with it from Allah, without altering it the least, just as (if) the king writes a written (instruction) and hands it over to his trustworthy (servant) and says (to him): Read it to so-and-so. Suyūṭī said: The Qur'ān belongs to the second kind, and the first kind is the *sunna*, and from this derives the reporting of the *sunna* according to the meaning unlike the Qur'ān.'[10]

9 For details see *kitāb al-risāla*, by Imām al-Shāfi'ī, Cairo, n.d., especially pp. 28-9. In English: Khadduri Majid, *Islamic Jurisprudence*. Shāfi'ī's Risala, Baltimore, 1961, chapter 5, especially pp. 121-2.

10 Ṣābūnī, *tibyān*, p.52.

It is generally accepted that the difference between Qur'ān and *sunna* is as follows:

The *aḥādīth* from or about the Prophet Muḥammad are:

— The words or actions of a human being, and not the speech of God as the Qur'ān is.
— Not necessarily reported in their precise wording, as the Qur'ān is.
— Not necessarily transmitted by *tawātur*, except in some instances.

Ḥadīth Qudsī[11]

Qudsī means holy, or pure. There are some reports from the Prophet Muḥammad where he relates to the people what God has said (says) or did (does), but this information is not part of the Qur'ān. Such a report is called *ḥadīth qudsī*, e.g.:

Abū Huraira reported that Allah's messenger said:

> 'Allah, Mighty and Exalted is He, said: If My servant likes to meet me, I like to meet him, and if he dislikes to meet Me, I dislike to meet him.'[12]

While the common factor between *ḥadīth qudsī* and the Qur'ān is that both contain words from Allah which have been revealed to Muḥammad, the main points of difference between Qur'ān and *ḥadīth qudsī* are as follows:

— In the Qur'ān the precise wording is from Allah, while in the *ḥadīth qudsī* the wording is given by the Prophet Muḥammad.
— The Qur'ān has been brought to Muḥammad only by the Angel Gabriel, while *ḥadīth qudsī* may also have been inspired otherwise, such as e.g. in a dream.

---

11 For an introduction to the subject and select sample texts, see e.g. Ibrahim, Izzuddin and Denis Johnson-Davies: *Forty Ḥadith Qudsi*, Beirut, Damascus, 1980.
12 *ibid.*, No. 30.

— The Qur'ān is inimitable and unique, but not so the *ḥadīth qudsī*.

— The Qur'ān has been transmitted by numerous persons, (*tawātur*) but the *ḥadīth* and *ḥadīth qudsī* often only by a few or even one individual. There are *ḥadīth qudsī* which are *ṣaḥīḥ*, but also others *ḥasan*, or even *ḍa'īf*, while there is no doubt at all about any *āya* from the Qur'ān.

Another point is that a *ḥadīth qudsī* cannot be recited in prayer.

Distinctive Features of the Qur'ān

The most important distinction between the Qur'ān and all other words or writings therefore is that the Qur'ān is the speech from Allah, revealed in its precise meaning and wording through the Angel Gabriel, transmitted by many, inimitable, unique and protected by Allah Himself against any corruption.

REVELATION AND HOW IT CAME TO THE PROPHET MUḤAMMAD

God guides His Creation

Allah the Creator has not only brought about the creation, but continues to sustain and direct it, in the way that He has created us and all that is around us. He has provided many forms of guidance, indeed, a system of guiding principles, of which the laws of 'nature' are a part.

But Allah has also granted a special form of guidance for mankind from the outset of its occupancy of the earth. He promised to Adam and his descendants: 'Get ye down all from here; and if, as is sure, there comes to you guidance from Me, whosoever follows guidance, on them shall be no fear, nor shall they grieve' (2:38).[13] This guidance comes through the prophets, whom Allah continuously sent to mankind, until the last messenger, Muḥammad received His final guidance.

Guidance through Revelation

We call a man to whom God in his own way communicates His guidance, a prophet or messenger (*nabī*, *rasūl*). Prophets receive the word of God through revelation and then communicate it to their fellow human beings:

> 'We have sent thee *inspiration*, as We sent it to Noah and the messengers after him: We sent *inspiration* to Abraham, Ismail, Isaac, Jacob and the tribes, to Jesus, Job, Jonah, Harun and Solomon, and to David We gave the Psalms. Of some apostles, We have already told the story, of others We have not – and to Moses God spoke direct – apostles who gave good news as well as warning, that mankind after (the coming) of the apostles should have no plea against God: for God is exalted in power and ways' (4:163-5).

The two words italicised in the above translation are both derived from the Arabic root '*waḥy*'.

The Meaning of Waḥy

The word *awḥā*, from which '*waḥy*' (revelation) is derived, occurs in a number of shades of meaning in the Qur'ān, each of them indicating the main underlying idea of inspiration directing or guiding someone. In each example below, the italicised words in the translation are forms of the root word *waḥy* in the original text of the Qur'ān:

— Guidance in natural intuition:
'so we sent this *inspiration* to the mother of Moses . . .' (28:7).

— Guidance in natural instinct:

---

13 The word here used for guidance is *hudan*.

'and thy Lord *taught* the bee to build its cells in hills, on trees and in (man's) habitations' (16: 68).

— Guidance by signs:
'So Zakaria came out to his people from his chamber: he *told* them *by signs* to celebrate God's praises in the morning and in the evening' (19: 11).

— Guidance from evil:
'Likewise did we make for every messenger an enemy – evil ones among men and jinns, *inspiring* each other with flowery discourses by way of deception . . .' (6: 112).

— Guidance from God:
'Remember thy Lord *inspired* the angels (with the message). . .' (8: 12).

Means of Revelation

Waḥy in the sense of 'revelation' is guidance from God for His creation, brought by the Prophets, who received the word from God through one of the means mentioned in the following Qur'ānic verse:

> 'It is not fitting for a man that God should speak to him except by inspiration, or from behind a veil, or by sending of a messenger to reveal with God's permission what God wills: for He is Most High, Most Wise' (42: 51).

Means of revelation are:

— Inspiration, e.g. in a dream (see 37: 102, where it is related that Ibrāhīm receives guidance in a vision, while asleep, to sacrifice his son).

— Speech hidden away (see 27: 8, where it is related that God spoke to Mūsā from the fire).

— Words (speech) sent through a special messenger from God (see 2: 97, where it is related that God sent the Angel Gabriel as the messenger to Muḥammad to reveal His message).

The Qur'ān revealed to Muḥammad

Prophet Muḥammad, the last of God's messengers, received the revelation of the Qur'ān through a special messenger sent by God for this purpose: the Angel Gabriel, who recited to him God's words exactly.

The Descent of the Qur'ān

According to Suyūṭī[14] on the basis of three reports from 'Abdullāh Ibn 'Abbās, in Ḥākim, Baihaqī and Nasā'ī, the Qur'ān descended in two stages:

— From the *lauḥ al-maḥfūẓ*, the 'well-preserved tablet', to the lowest of the heavens *(bait al-'izza)* of the world, all together, in the *laila al-qadr.*

— From the heavens to earth in stages throughout the twenty-three years of Muḥammad's prophethood, and first in the *laila al-qadr* of Ramaḍān, through the Angel Gabriel.

This second descent from the heaven to the heart of the Prophet is referred to in *Sūra al-isrā'* (17) and *Sūra al-furqān* (25).

BEGINNING OF THE REVELATION

The revelation of the Qur'ān began in the *laila al-qadr* of Ramaḍān (the 27th night or one of the odd nights after the 21st) after the Prophet Muḥammad had passed the fortieth year of his life (that is around the year 610), during his seclusion in the cave of Ḥirā' on a mountain near Makka.

---

14 *al-itqān fī 'ulūm al-qur'ān*, Beirut, 1973, Vol. I, pp.39-40.

Bukhārī's[15] Account

This is the account, as reported in the *Ṣaḥīḥ* of Bukhārī:

> Narrated Aisha the mother of the faithful believers: The commencement of the divine inspiration to Allah's apostle was in the form of good dreams which came like bright daylight (i.e. true) and then the love of seclusion was bestowed upon him.
>
> He used to go in seclusion in the Cave of Ḥirā', where he used to worship (Allah alone) continuously for many days before his desire to see his family. He used to take with him food for the stay and then come back to (his wife) Khadīja to take his food likewise again, till suddenly the truth descended upon him while he was in the Cave of Hirā'.
>
> The angel came to him and asked him to read. The Prophet replied 'I do not know how to read'.
>
> The Prophet added, 'The angel caught me (forcibly) and pressed me so hard that I could not bear it any more. He then released me and again asked me to read and I replied, "I do not know how to read". Thereupon he caught me again and pressed me a second time till I could not bear it any more. He then released me and again asked me to read, but again I replied, "I do not know how to read" (or what shall I read?). Thereupon he caught me for the third time and pressed me, and then released me and said: "Read, in the name of Your Lord, who created, created man from a clot. Read! And Your Lord is the most bountiful"'.[16]

The narration goes on to tell us that the Prophet went back to his wife Khadīja and recounted to her his dreadful experience. She comforted him and both of them consulted Waraqa, Khadīja's relative and a learned Christian, about it. Waraqa

---

15 English translations of *aḥādīth* are, unless otherwise indicated, from Khan, Muhammad Muhsin: *The Translation of the Meanings of Saḥih al-Bukhari*, 9 vols., Istanbul, 1978 (abbr. as Bukhārī) and Siddiqui, Abdul Ḥamid: *Saḥih Muslim*, 4 vols., Lahore, 1978 (abbr. as Muslim).

16 Bukhārī, I, No. 3; VI, No. 478; Muslim I, No. 301.

told Muḥammad that he had encountered the one 'whom Allah had sent to Moses' and that he would be driven out by his people.

How Revelation came

> Narrated Aisha, the mother of the faithful believers: Al-Ḥārith bin Hishām asked Allah's apostle: 'O Allah's apostle! How is the divine inspiration revealed to you?' Allah's apostle replied, 'Sometimes it is "revealed" like the ringing of a bell, this form of inspiration is the hardest of all and then this state passes off after I have grasped what is inspired. Sometimes the Angel comes in the form of a man and talks to me and I grasp whatever he says'.[17]

The First Revelation[18]

The first revelation that the Prophet Muḥammad received is in the first verses from *Sūra al-'alaq* (96: 1-3, according to others 1-5):

> 'Read in the name of your Lord, who created, created man from a clot. Read! And your Lord is most bountiful. (He who taught) the use of the pen taught man which he knew not.'

The remainder of *Sūra* 96, which now has 19 *āyāt*, was revealed on some later occasion.

The Pause (*fatra*)

After the first message thus received, revelation ceased for a certain period (called *fatra*) and then resumed:

> Narrated Jābir bin 'Abdullāh Al-Anṣārī while talking about the period of pause in revelation reporting the speech of the Prophet, 'While I was walking, all of a

17 Bukhārī, I, No. 2.
18 See Suyūṭī, *itqān*, I, pp.23-4.

sudden I heard a voice from the heaven. I looked up and saw the same angel who had visited me at the Cave of Ḥira' sitting on a chair between the sky and the earth. I got afraid of him and came back home and said "Wrap me (in blankets)" and then Allah revealed the following holy verses (of the Qur'ān): O you covered in your cloak, arise and warn (the people against Allah's punishment) . . . up to "and all pollution shun".'

After this revelation came strongly and regularly.[19]

The Second Revelation

The second portion of the Qur'ān revealed to the Prophet Muḥammad was the beginning of *Sūra al-muddaththir* (74: 1-5). It now consists of 56 verses, the rest revealed later, and begins as follows: 'O you, covered in your cloak, arise and warn, thy Lord magnify, thy raiment purify, pollution shun...'

Other Early Revelations

Many hold that *Sūra al-muzzammil* (73) was the next revelation.

According to others, *Sūra al-fātiḥa* (1) was the third *sūra* to be revealed.[20]

Among other early revelations, which the Prophet declared in Makka, are, according to some reports, *Sūra* 111, *Sūra* 81, *Sūra* 87, *Sūra* 92, *Sūra* 89, etc. Then revelation continued, 'mentioning Paradise and Hell, and until mankind turned to Islam, then came revelation about ḥalāl and ḥarām. . .'[21]

Revelation came to the Prophet throughout his lifetime, both in Makka and Madina, i.e. over a period of approximately 23 years, until shortly before his death in the year 10 after *Hijra* (632).

---

19 Bukhārī, I, end of No. 3.
20 Suyūṭī, *itqān,* I, p.24.
21 *ibid.*

The Last Revelation

Many Muslim scholars agree that the last revelation was *Sūra* 2, verse 281:

> 'And fear the day when ye shall be brought back to God. Then shall every soul be paid what it earned and none shall be dealt with unjustly.'

Some also say that it was 2: 282 or 2: 278.[22]

It has also been suggested that all three verses were revealed on one occasion. The Prophet died nine nights after the last revelation.

Others hold that *Sūra* 5: 4 was the last to be revealed:

> 'This day I have perfected your religion for you, completed My favour upon you and have chosen for you Islam as your religion.'

The opinion that this verse was the last revelation is not sound according to many scholars, since it was revealed during the last pilgrimage of the Prophet. This information is based upon a *ḥadīth* from 'Umar. Suyūṭī explains concerning the verse in *Sūra* 5 that after it nothing concerning *aḥkām* and *ḥalāl* and *ḥarām* was revealed, and in this sense it is the 'completion' of religion. However, revelation reminding man of the coming day of judgement continued and the last such revelation is the above verse.[23]

Reasons why the Qur'ān was sent down in Stages

The Qur'ān was revealed in stages over a period of 23 years, and not as a complete book in one single act of revelation. There are a number of reasons for this; most important are the following:

— To strengthen the heart of the Prophet by addressing him continuously and whenever the need for guidance arose.

---

22 Kamāl, Ahmad 'Adil: *'ulūm al-qur'ān*, Cairo, 1974, p.18.
23 Ṣābūnī, *tibyān*, pp.18-9.

— Out of consideration for the Prophet since revelation was a very difficult experience for him.
— To gradually implement the laws of God.
— To make understanding, application and memorisation of the revelation easier for the believers.

CHAPTER 2

Transmission of the Qur'ānic Revelation

The revelation contained in the Qur'ān has been transmitted to us by numerous persons in two ways: orally and in written form.

MEMORISATION AND ORAL TRANSMISSION

Memorisation by the Prophet

Oral transmission of the revelation was based on *ḥifẓ* or memorisation and the Prophet Muḥammad himself was the first to commit a revelation to memory after the Angel Gabriel had brought it to him:

> 'Move not thy tongue concerning the (Qur'ān) to make haste therewith. It is for Us to collect it and promulgate it; but when We have promulgated it, follow thou its recital' (75: 16-19).
>
> '. . . an apostle from God, rehearsing scriptures, kept pure and holy . . .' (98: 2).

Memorisation by the Companions

The Prophet then declared the revelation and instructed his Companions to memorise it. The case of Ibn Mas'ūd, who was the first man to publicly recite the Qur'ān in Makka, shows that even in the very early phase of the Islamic *umma* recital of the revelation from memory was practised by the Companions:

'. . . the first man to speak the Qur'ān loudly in Makka after the apostle was 'Abdullāh bin Mas'ūd. The Prophet's Companions came together and mentioned that the Quraish had never heard the Qur'ān distinctly read to them . . . When (Ibn Mas'ūd) arrived at the *maqām*, he read "In the name of God the Compassionate the Merciful", raising his voice as he did so. "The Compassionate who taught the Qur'ān . . ." (55: 1). . .They got up and began to hit him in the face; but he continued to read so far as God willed that he should read. . .'[1]

It is also reported that Abū Bakr used to recite the Qur'ān publicly in front of his house in Makka.[2]

The Prophet encourages Memorisation

There are numerous *aḥādīth*, giving account of various efforts made and measures taken by the Prophet to ensure that the revelation was preserved in the memory of his Companions. The following is perhaps the most clear:

'Narrated 'Uthmān bin 'Affān: The Prophet said: "The most superior among you (Muslims) are those who learn the Qur'ān and teach it".'[3]

It is also well known that the recital of the Qur'ān during the daily prayers is required and hence many Companions heard repeatedly passages from the revelation, memorised them and used them in prayer.

The Prophet also listened to the recitation of the Qur'ān by the Companions.

Narrated 'Abdullāh (b. Mas'ud): 'Allah's Apostle said to me: "Recite (of the Qur'ān) for me". I said: "Shall I recite it to you although it had been revealed to you?!" He said: "I like to hear (the Qur'ān) from others". So I

---

1 Guillaume, E.: *The Life of Muhammad* (abbr. as *Ibn Hishām*), London, 1955, pp.141-2; Ibn Hishām: *Sīra al-nabī*, Cairo, n.d., I, p.206.

2 *Sīra* Ibn Hishām, *ibid.*

3 Bukhārī, VI, No. 546.

> recited Sūrat-an-Nisā' till I reached: "How (will it be) then when We bring from each nation a witness and We bring you (O Muḥammad) as a witness against these people?"' (4:41).

'Then he said: "Stop!" Behold, his eyes were shedding tears then.'[4]

The Prophet sent Teachers

The Prophet sent teachers to communities in other places so that they might receive instruction in Islam and the Qur'ān.

The case of Muṣ'ab bin 'Umair illustrates that this was so even before the *hijra*:

> 'When these men (of the first pledge of 'Aqaba) left (for Madina) the apostle sent with them Muṣ'ab bin 'Umair . . . and instructed him to read the Qur'ān to them and to teach them Islam and to give them instruction about religion. In Madina Muṣ'ab was called "the reader".'[5]

Another well-known case concerns Mu'ādh bin Jabal who was sent to Yemen to instruct the people there.

Qur'ān Readers among the Companions

Suyūṭī[6] mentions more than twenty well-known persons who memorised the revelation, among them were Abū Bakr, 'Umar, 'Uthmān, 'Alī, Ibn Mas'ūd, Abū Huraira, 'Abdullāh bin 'Abbās, 'Abdullāh bin 'Amr bin al-'Āṣ, 'Ā'isha, Ḥafṣa, and Umm Salama.

From among these, the Prophet himself recommended especially the following:

> 'Narrated Masrūq: 'Abdullāh bin 'Amr mentioned 'Abdullāh bin Mas'ūd and said: I shall ever love that man for I heard the Prophet saying: Take (learn) the Qur'ān

---

4 Bukhārī, VI, No. 106.
5 Ibn Hishām, p.199.
6 *Itqān*, I, p.124.

from four: 'Abdullāh bin Mas'ūd, Sālim, Mu'ādh and Ubay bin Ka'b'.[7]

Another *ḥadīth* informs us about those Companions who had memorised the Qur'ān in its entirety and gone over it with the Prophet before his death:

> 'Narrated Qatāda: I asked Anas bin Mālik: Who collected the Qur'ān at the time of the Prophet? He replied, Four, all of whom were from the Anṣār: Ubay bin Ka'b, Mu'ādh bin Jabal, Zaid bin Thābit and Abū Zaid.'[8]

The fact that some of the earliest historical reports make special mention in the accounts of the battles that were fought, of Muslims killed who knew (something of) the Qur'ān by heart, gives a clear indication that memorisation of the revelation was considered important and widely practised from the earliest times.[9]

The Qur'ān Memorised in the Prophet's Lifetime

It is therefore certain that the Qur'ān had been memorised by the Companions of the Prophet during his lifetime. This tradition continued among the Companions after the Prophet's death and, later, among the *tābi'ūn* and all generations of Muslims that have followed, until today.

TRANSMISSION OF THE WRITTEN TEXT

The Written Text at the Time of the Prophet Muḥammad

What is meant by Jam' al-Qur'ān?

The general meaning of *jam' al-qur'ān* is to 'bring together

7 Bukhārī, VI, No. 521.
8 Bukhārī, VI, No. 525.
9 See below, on collection of the Qur'ān in Abū Bakr's time.

the Qur'ān'. This was done and has to be understood in two ways:

— Bringing together the Qur'ān orally, or in one's mind (*ḥifẓ*).
— Bringing together the Qur'ān in written form, or on sheets, or in a book.

Jam' al-qur'ān therefore, in the classical literature, has various meanings:

— To learn the Qur'ān by heart.
— To write down every revelation.
— To bring together those materials upon which the Qur'ān has been written.
— To bring together the reports of people who have memorised the Qur'ān.
— To bring together all such sources, both oral and written.

How was the Qur'ān Collected?

In Suyūṭī's *itqān* it is said that the Qur'ān had been written down in its entirety in the time of the Prophet but had not been brought together in one single place, and that therefore these written records or documents had not been arranged in order.[10]

However, this statement does not preclude that the ordering of the Qur'ān and the arrangement of the *sūras*, was fixed by the Prophet himself and safeguarded through oral transmission.

Stages of Collection

As far as the written text is concerned, one may distinguish three stages:

1 In the time of the Prophet:

10 *Itqān*, I, p.41.

— in the hearts of men (memorisation).
— on writing materials.

2 In the time of Abū Bakr.

3 In the time of 'Uthmān.

Why was no Book left by the Prophet?

The Prophet Muḥammad did not present to his Companions the revelation collected and arranged in a single written volume. There are a number of good reasons for this:

— Because the revelation did not come down in one piece, but at intervals and was received continuously until the end of the Prophet's life.

— Because some verses were abrogated in the course of revelation, and therefore flexibility needed to be maintained.

— The *āyāt* and *sūras* were not always revealed in their final order, but were arranged later.

— The Prophet lived only nine days after the last revelation and was severely ill.

— There was no dispute or friction about the Qur'ān during the time of the Prophet, as developed afterwards when he, as the final authority, was no longer available.

Writing down the Revelation

While writing was not widespread among the people in Arabia at the time of the Prophet there were persons of whom it is reported that they did write. It is said for example of Waraqa, Khadīja's cousin, that he had been converted to Christianity in the pre-Islamic period 'and used to write Arabic and write of the Gospel in Arabic as much as Allah wished him to write'.[11]

The Prophet himself did much to encourage the Muslims to learn to write. It is related that some of the Quraish, who were

11 Bukhārī, VI, No. 478.

taken prisoners at the battle of Badr, regained their freedom after they had taught some of the Muslims the art of writing.[12]

Did the Prophet himself write?

Although it is not clear whether the Prophet Muḥammad knew how to write, there is unanimous agreement among scholars that Muḥammad himself did not write down the revelation. The Qur'ān clearly states:

> 'And thou (O Muḥammad) wast not a reader of any scripture before it, nor didst thou write it with thy right hand, for then might those have doubted who follow falsehood' (29: 48).

The Qur'ān also refers to Muḥammad on several occasions as the 'unlettered prophet' which some scholars have interpreted in the sense that he did not read or write:

> 'Those who follow the apostle, the unlettered prophet . . .' (8: 157).

His community too has been described as 'unlettered':

> 'It is he who has sent amongst the unlettered an apostle from among themselves. . .' (62: 2).

The Qur'ān written during the Prophet's Lifetime

There is no doubt that the Qur'ān was not only transmitted orally by many Muslims who had learned parts or the whole of it, but that it was also written down during the lifetime of the Prophet.

The well-known report about 'Umar's conversion shows that large passages of the revelation had already been written down even at a very early time, in Makka, long before the *hijra*, when the Prophet was still in the house of Arqam. 'Umar had set out to kill the Prophet Muḥammad, when somebody informed him that Islam had already spread into

---

12 *Ṭabaqāt* Ibn Sa'd, II (2), p.19.

his own family and pointed out to him that his brother-in-law, his nephew and his sister had all become Muslims. 'Umar went to the house of his sister and found her together with her husband and another Muslim. A dispute arose and 'Umar violently attacked both his brother-in-law and his own sister. 'When he did that they said to him "Yes, we are Muslims and we believe in God and His apostle and you can do what you like".' When 'Umar saw the blood on his sister, he was sorry for what he had done and turned back and said to his sister, 'Give me this sheet which I heard you reading just now so that I may see just what it is which Muḥammad has brought', for 'Umar could write. When he said that, his sister replied that she was afraid to trust him with it. 'Do not be afraid', he said and he swore by his gods that he would return it when he had read it. When he said that, she had hopes that he would become a Muslim and said to him, 'My brother, you are unclean in your polytheism and only the clean may touch it'. So 'Umar rose and washed himself and she gave him the page in which was Ṭāhā and when he had read the beginning he said 'How fine and noble is this speech . . .'[13]

The Qur'ān Dictated by the Prophet

The Qur'ān was not only written down by those Companions who did so on their own initiative. Indeed, the Prophet, when a revelation came, called for the scribe and dictated to him. The Prophet while in Madina had several such scribes,[14] among whom Zaid bin Thābit was very prominent.

> Narrated al-Barā': There was revealed 'Not equal are those believers who sit (at home) and those who strive and fight in the cause of Allah' (4:95). The Prophet said: 'Call Zaid for me and let him bring the board, the ink pot and the scapula bone (or the scapula bone and the ink pot).' Then he said: 'Write: Not equal are those believers . . .'[15]

---

13 Ibn Hishām, pp. 156-7.

14 M. M. A'zami, in his book *Kuttāb al-Nabī* (Beirut, 1393/1974) mentions 48 persons who used to write for the Prophet.

15 Bukhārī, VI, No. 512; also VI, No. 116-18.

It is also reported that material upon which the revelation had been written down was kept in the house of the Prophet.[16]

Written during the Prophet's Lifetime

Another report informs us that when people came to Madina to learn about Islam, they were provided with 'copies of the chapters of the Qur'ān, to read and learn them by heart'.[17]

Further evidence for the existence of the Qur'ān as a written document during the lifetime of the Prophet comes from the following account:

> 'Abd Allāh b. Abū Bakr b. Ḥazm reported: The book written by the apostle of Allah for 'Amr b. Ḥazm contained also this that no man should touch the Qur'ān without ablution.[18]
>
> The book, which Allah's messenger wrote for 'Amr b. Ḥazm that no one should touch the Qur'ān except the purified one:
>
> Mālik said: And no one should carry the *muṣḥaf* by its strap, nor on a pillow, unless he is clean. And even if this be allowed to carry it in its cover, it is not disliked, if there is not in the two hands which carry it, something polluting the *muṣḥaf*, but it is disliked for the one who carries it, and he is not clean, in honour to the Qur'ān and respect to it. Mālik said: The best I heard about this is the verse 'None shall touch it but those who are clean' (56: 79).[19]

The commentary to the *muwaṭṭa'* explains that the book referred to as written by the Prophet (which means of course written upon his instruction) was sent with some Muslims for instruction in Islam of the people of Yemen.[20]

---

16 Suyūṭī, *itqān*, I, p.58.
17 Ḥamīdullah, M.: *Saḥīfa Hammām ibn Munabbih,* Paris, 1979, p.64.
18 *Muwaṭṭa'*, No. 462.
19 *Muwaṭṭa'*, Arabic, p.204.
20 *ibid.*

In fact the Qur'ānic verse 56:79, read in context, clearly explains that the Qur'ān is available to those who receive instruction by revelation, in the form of a book or a piece of writing:

> '. . . this is indeed a Qur'ān most honourable, in a book (*kitāb*) well guarded, which none shall touch but those who are clean: a revelation from the Lord of the worlds' (56:77-80).

The same fact, i.e. that the Qur'ān did exist as a written document in the lifetime of the Prophet is proved by the following *aḥādīth*:

> From Ibn 'Umar: . . . 'The messenger of Allah (may peace be upon him) said: "Do not take the Qur'ān on a journey with you, for I am afraid lest it should fall into the hands of the enemy"'.[21]

The correctness of the assumption that the reference is to a *written document* is supported by one of the transmitters: Ayyūb (i.e. one of the narrators in the chain of transmission of this report) said: The enemy may seize it and may quarrel with you over it.[22]

Furthermore, the chapter-heading used by Bukhārī for the section, (which usually contains additional information,) explains:

> 'Ibn 'Umar said: No doubt the Prophet and his Companions travelled in the land of the enemy and they knew the Qur'ān then.'[23]

Collection of Revelation during the Prophet's Lifetime

During his last pilgrimage, at the sermon which he gave to the large gathering of Muslims, the Prophet said: 'I have left with you something which if you will hold fast to it you will

---

21 Muslim, III, No. 4609, also 4607, 4608; Bukhārī, IV, No. 233.

22 Muslim, III, No. 4609.

23 i.e. they knew that the Qur'ān was carried – as a scripture – by the Muslims. Bukhārī, IV, p.146, Ch.129.

never fall into error – a plain indication, the book of God and the practice of his prophet. . .'[24]

This advice from the Prophet to the Muslims implies that the revelation was available as *kitāb* (writing) before his death, for otherwise he would have referred to it in some other term.

From other reports also, we can conclude that the Prophet himself took care of the actual arrangement of the revelation, when it was written down.

Zaid is reported to have said:

> 'We used to compile the Qur'ān from small scraps in the presence of the Apostle.'[25]

'Uthmān said, that in later days, the Prophet 'used to, when something was revealed to him, call someone from among those who used to write for him and said: Place these āyāt in the sūra, in which this and this is mentioned, and when (only) one āya was revealed to him, he said: Place this āya in the sūra in which this and this is mentioned'.[26]

This indicates that not only was the revelation written down during the lifetime of the Prophet, but that he himself gave instructions for the arrangement of the material. According to some other reports, it is also clear, that this proper arrangement and order of the *āyāt* was well known to the Companions of the Prophet, and they were not prepared to tamper with it.

> 'Narrated Ibn Az-Zubair: I said to 'Uthmān "This verse which is in Sūra al-Baqara: 'those of you who die and leave wives behind . . . without turning them out' has been abrogated by another verse. Why then do you write it in the Qur'ān?" 'Uthmān said: Leave it (where it is) O son of my brother, for I will not shift anything of it (i.e. the Qur'ān) from its original position.'[27]

Similarly quite a number of reports mention the various

---

24 Ibn Hishām, p.651.

25 *Itqān*, I, p.99; Ṣāliḥ, p.69.

26 Jeffery, A.: *Materials for the history of the text of the Qur'ān*, (incl. *Kitāb al-maṣāḥif* by Ibn Abī Dāwūd (abbr. as Ibn Abī Dāwūd, *maṣāḥif*), Leiden, 1937, p.31.

27 Bukhārī, VI. No. 60.

Sūras by their names or beginnings. Two examples may suffice to make this point:

> Narrated Abū Huraira: The Prophet used to recite the following in the Fajr prayer of Friday: *Alif Lām Mīm Tanzīl* (*Sajda*) (32) and *Hal-atā 'ala-l-Insāni* (*al-dahr*) (76).[28]
>
> Abu Huraira said: God's messenger recited in both rak'as of the dawn prayer: "Say O unbelievers (99) and Say, He is God, one God (112)".'[29]

The order and arrangement was of course well known to the Muslims due to the daily recitation of the Qur'ān in the prayers at the mosque of the Prophet and at other places. Finally there are three *aḥādīth* in *Ṣaḥīḥ* Bukhārī, informing us that the Angel Gabriel used to recite the Qur'ān with the Prophet once a year, but he recited it twice with him in the year he died. The Prophet used to stay in *i'tikāf* for ten days every year (in the month of Ramaḍān), but in the year of his death, he stayed in *i'tikāf* for twenty days.[30]

We can therefore distinguish the following measures which ensured the collection of the revelation in writing during the lifetime of the Prophet:

— Revelation used to be written down even in the very early days of the Prophet's call.

— In Madina, the Prophet had several persons who wrote down revelation when it was revealed.

— The Prophet himself instructed his scribes as to where the different revealed verses should be placed, and thus determined the order and arrangement.

— This order and arrangement was well known to the Muslims and strictly observed by them.

— The Angel Gabriel went through all the revelation with Muḥammad each year in Ramaḍān, and went through it twice in the year the Prophet died.

---

28 Bukhārī, II, No. 16.

29 Robson, J. (transl.): *Mishkāt al Maṣābīḥ*, Lahore, 1963, I, pp. 172-3; Tabrīzī: *Mishkāt al-maṣābīh*, Beirut, 1961, I, No. 842.

30 Bukhārī, VI, No. 520; see also Nos. 518, 519.

— There are numerous reports about the existence of the written Qur'ān – in the form of a book or piece of writing (*kitāb*) during the lifetime of the Prophet.

What did the Prophet leave behind?

The way the material of revelation was left by the Prophet at his death was the most suitable for the Companions in that:

— All parts of the revelation were available both in written form and memorised by the Companions.
— All pieces were available on loose writing material, making it easy to arrange them in the proper order.
— The order already fixed of the *āyāt* within the *sūras*, in the written form, as well as in the memory of the Companions, and of the *sūras* in the memory of the Companions.

What arrangement could have been better than to have everything to hand in written form, as well as memorised by the Muslims, and to have the order and arrangement already determined, partially in the written form and completely in the memories of the people?

It is for these reasons that a later scholar, al-Hārith al-Muḥāsibī in his book *kitāb fahm al-Sunan*, summarised the first phase of the written collection of the Qur'ānic material in the following words:

> 'Writing of the Qur'ān was no novelty, for the Prophet used to order that it be written down, but it was in separate pieces, on scraps of leather, shoulder blades and palm risp, and when (Abū Bakr) al-Ṣiddīq ordered that it be copied from the (various) places to a common place, which was in the shape of sheets, these (materials) were found in the house of the Prophet in which the Qur'ān was spread out, and he gathered it all together and tied it with a string so that nothing of it was lost.'[31]

It is obvious that the history of the Qur'ānic text

31 Suyūṭī, *itqān*, I, p.58.

(Textgeschichte) cannot be compared with that of other Holy Scriptures. While the books of the Old and New Testaments, for example, were written, edited and compiled over long periods, sometimes centuries, the text of the Qur'ān, once revelation had ceased, has remained the same to this day.

Ṣuḥuf and Muṣḥaf

Both words are derived from the same root *Ṣaḥafa* 'to write'. The word *ṣuḥuf* also occurs in the Qur'ān (87:19) meaning scripture or written sheets.

Ṣuḥuf (sg. *ṣaḥīfa*) means loose pieces of writing material, such as paper, skin, papyrus, etc.

Muṣḥaf (pl. *maṣāḥif*) means the collected *ṣuḥuf*, brought together into a fixed order, such as between two covers, into a volume.

In the history of the written text of the Qur'ān, *ṣuḥuf* stands for the sheets on which the Qur'ān was collected in the time of Abū Bakr. In these *ṣuḥuf* the order of the *āyāt* within each *sūra* was fixed, but the sheets with the *sūras* on them were still in a loose arrangement, i.e. not bound into a volume.

Muṣḥaf in the present context means the sheets on which the Qur'ān was collected in the time of 'Uthmān. Here both the order of the *āyāt* within each *sūra* as well as the order of the sheets were fixed.

Today we also call any copy of the Qur'ān, which has both order of *āyāt* and *sūras* fixed, a *muṣḥaf*.

How the Ṣuḥuf were made

Tradition informs us that at the Battle of Yamāma (11/633), in the time of Abū Bakr, a number of Muslims, who had memorised the Qur'ān were killed. Hence it was feared that unless a written copy of the Qur'ān were prepared, a large part of the revelation might be lost.

The following is the account in the *Ṣaḥīḥ* Bukhārī:

> Narrated Zaid bin Thābit Al-Anṣārī, one of the scribes of the Revelation: Abū Bakr sent for me after the casualties among the warriors (of the battle) of Yamāma (where

a great number of Qurrā were killed). 'Umar was present with Abū Bakr who said: "Umar has come to me and said, the People have suffered heavy casualties on the day of (the battle of) Yamāma, and I am afraid that there will be some casualties among the Qurrā (those who know the Qur'ān by heart) at other places, whereby a large part of the Qur'ān may be lost, unless you collect it. And I am of the opinion that you should collect the Qur'ān.' Abū Bakr added, 'I said to 'Umar, "How can I do something which Allāh's Apostle has not done?" 'Umar said (to me) "By Allāh, it is (really) a good thing". So 'Umar kept on pressing trying to persuade me to accept his proposal, till Allāh opened my bosom for it and I had the same opinion as 'Umar'. (Zaid bin Thābit added:) 'Umar was sitting with him (Abū Bakr) and was not speaking. Abū Bakr said (to me), 'You are a wise young man and we do not suspect you (of telling lies or of forgetfulness); and you used to write the Divine Inspiration for Allāh's Apostle. Therefore, look for the Qur'ān and collect it (in one manuscript)'. By Allāh, if he (Abū Bakr) had ordered me to shift one of the mountains (from its place) it would not have been harder for me than what he had ordered me concerning the collection of the Qur'ān. I said to both of them, 'How dare you do a thing which the Prophet has not done?' Abū Bakr said, 'By Allāh, it is (really) a good thing. So I kept on arguing with him about it till Allāh opened my bosom for that which He had opened the bosoms of Abū Bakr and 'Umar. So I started locating the Quranic material and collecting it from parchments, scapula, leafstalks of date palms and from the memories of men (who knew it by heart). I found with Khuzaima two verses of Sūra at-Tauba which I had not found with anybody else (and they were):

> 'Verily there has come to you an Apostle (Muḥammad) from among yourselves. It grieves him that you should receive any injury or difficulty. He (Muḥammad) is ardently anxious over you (to be rightly guided)' (9: 128).

The manuscript on which the Qur'ān was collected, remained with Abū Bakr till Allah took him unto Him, and then with 'Umar till Allah took him unto Him, and finally it remained with Ḥafṣa, 'Umar's daughter.[32]

Here we can distinguish the following steps, which led to the preparation of the *ṣuḥuf*:

— Zaid was instructed by Abū Bakr to collect the Qur'ān.

— Zaid collected it from various written materials and the memories of people.

— The sheets thus prepared were kept with Abū Bakr, then 'Umar, then Ḥafṣa.

THE MAṢĀḤIF OF THE COMPANIONS

There are numerous indications in the literature of *ḥadīth* that several of the Companions of the Prophet had prepared their own written collections of the revelations.[33] The best-known among these are from Ibn Mas'ūd, Ubay bin Ka'b and Zaid bin Thābit.[34]

A list of Companions of whom it is related that they had their own written collections included the following: Ibn Mas'ūd, Ubay bin Ka'b, 'Alī, Ibn 'Abbās, Abū Mūsā, Ḥafṣa, Anas bin Mālik, 'Umar, Zaid bin Thābit, Ibn Al-Zubair, 'Abdullāh ibn 'Amr, 'Ā'isha, Sālim, Umm Salama, 'Ubaid bin 'Umar.[35]

It is also known that 'Ā'isha and Ḥafṣa had their own scripts

---

32 Bukhārī, VI, No. 201.

33 Suyūṭī, *itqān*, I, p.62.

34 See Dodge, B.: *The Fihrist of al-Nadim*, New York, 1970 (abbr. as *fihrist*), pp. 53-63.

35 See Ibn Abī Dawūd: *Maṣāḥif*, p.14. Anṣari, M.: *The Qur'ānic Foundations and Structure of Muslim Society*, Karachi, 1973, drawing upon various sources, says (I, p.76, note 2) that there existed at least 15 written copies of the Qur'ān in the Prophet's lifetime. In addition to the list of 15 names quoted above, he includes Abū Bakr, 'Uthmān, Mu'adh b. Jabal, Abū Dardā', Abū Ayyūb Anṣārī, 'Ubāda b. al-Ṣāmit, Tamīm Dari. This would add up to 23 written copies of the Qur'ān, which existed while the Prophet was alive.

written after the Prophet had died.[36]

The following is a very brief description of some of the *maṣāḥif*, which are attributed to the Companions of the Prophet. All the information is based on classical sources.[37]

The Muṣḥaf of Ibn Mas'ūd (d. 33/653)

He wrote a muṣḥaf, in which *sūras* 1, 113 and 114 were not included. Ibn al-Nadīm[38] however said he had seen a copy of the Qur'ān from Ibn Mas'ūd which did not contain *al-fātiḥa* (*Sūra* 1). The arrangement of the *sūras* differed from the 'Uthmānic text. The following is the order attributed to Ibn Mas'ūd's copy:[39]

2, 4, 3, 7, 6, 5, 10, 9, 16, 11, 12, 17, 21, 23, 26, 37, 33, 28, 24, 8, 19, 29, 30, 36, 25, 22, 13, 34, 35, 14, 38, 47, 31, 35, 40, 43, 41, 46, 45, 44, 48, 57, 59, 32, 50, 65, 49, 67, 64, 63, 62, 61, 72, 71, 58, 60, 66, 55, 53, 51, 52, 54, 69, 56, 68, 79, 70, 73, 74, 83, 80, 76, 75, 77, 78, 81, 82, 88, 87, 92, 89, 85, 84, 96, 90, 93, 94, 86, 100, 107, 101, 98, 91, 95, 104, 105, 106, 102, 97, 110, 108, 109, 111, 112.

This list is obviously incomplete. It contains only 106 *sūras* and not 110, as Ibn Nadīm wrote.

In *Sūra al-baqara,* which I take as an example, there are a total of 101 variants. Most of them concern spelling, some also choice of words (synonyms), use of particles, etc.

Examples:

Pronunciation:

2: 70	Ibn Mas'ūd reads	*al-baqira*
	in place of	*al-baqara*

Spelling:

2: 19	He reads	*kulla mā*
	in place of	*kullamā*

---

36 Rahimuddin, M. (transl.): *Muwattā Imam Malik,* Lahore, 1980, No. 307, 308; Mālik b. Anas: *al-muwaṭṭa'*, Cairo, n.d., p. 105.

37 For details see Ibn Abī Dawūd, also *fihrist* and *itqān*.

38 *Fihrist*, I, pp. 57-8.

39 *Fihrist*, I, pp. 53-7.

Synonyms:

2: 68	He reads in place of	*sal* (seek, beseech) *ud'u* (beseech)

Assuming that all these are reliable reports, the copy of Ibn Mas'ūd would then have been prepared for his personal use and written before all 114 *sūras* were revealed.

Nadīm, who lived in the tenth century (4th century *Hijra*) also added: 'I have seen a number of Qur'ānic manuscripts, which the transcribers recorded as manuscripts of Ibn Mas'ūd. No two of the Qur'ānic copies were in agreement and most of them were on badly effaced parchment . . .'[40]

This note indicates that the question of authentic manuscripts of Ibn Mas'ūd needs to be treated with some caution.

The Muṣḥaf of Ubay bin Ka'b (d. 29 H/649)

He wrote a *muṣḥaf*, in which two 'additional *sūras* and another 'additional *āya*' were reportedly found.[41]

---

40 *Fihrist*, I, p.57.

41 *Itqān*, I, p.65; Ibn Abī Dāwūd, *maṣāḥif*, pp. 180-1; also Noldeke, T. et al.: *Geschichte des Qorans*, Leipzig, 1909-38 (abbr. as GdQ), II, pp.33-8. The first so-called *sūra* entitled *al-khal'* (separation), translates as follows: 'O Allah, we seek your help and ask your forgiveness, and we praise you and we do not disbelieve in you. We separate from and leave who sins against you.'

The second so-called *sūra*, entitled *al-ḥafd* (haste) translates as follows: 'O Allah, we worship You and to You we pray and prostrate and to You we run and hasten to serve You. We hope for Your mercy and we fear Your punishment. Your punishment will certainly reach the disbelievers.'

Obviously these two pieces constitute so-called *'qunūt'*, i.e. supplications which the Prophet sometimes said in the morning prayer or *witr* prayer after recitation of *sūras* from the Qur'ān. They are in fact identical to some parts of *qunūt* reported in the collections of *ḥadīth*. See: Nawawī, *al-adhkār*, Cairo, 1955, pp.57-8.

As to the single additional so-called *āya*, its translation is as follows: 'If the son of Adam was given a valley full of riches, he would wish a second one, and if he was given two valleys full of riches, he would surely ask for a third one. Nothing will fill the belly of the son of Adam except dust, and Allah is forgiving to him who is repentant.'

Again this text is known to be a *ḥadīth* from the Prophet. See Bukhārī, VIII, No. 444-47. According to Ibn 'Abbās (No. 445) and 'Ubay (No. 446) this text was at times thought to be part of the Qur'ān. However Ubay himself clarifies that after *Sūra* 102: 1 had been revealed, they (i.e. the *ṣaḥāba*) did not consider the above to be part of the Qur'ān. See Bukhārī, VIII, No. 446. This explanation of Ubay also makes it very clear that the Companions did not differ at all about what was part of the Qur'ān

The order of the *sūras* is again different from 'Uthmān as well as Ibn Mas'ūd.

The following is the order of *sūras* in the copy attributed to Ubay b. Ka'b:[42]

1, 2, 4, 3, 6, 7, 5, 10, 8, 9, 11, 19, 26, 22, 12, 18, 16, 33, 17, 39, 45, 20, 21, 24, 23, 40, 13, 28, 27, 37, 38, 36, 15, 42, 30, 43, 41, 14, 35, 48, 47, 57, 52, 25, 32, 71, 46, 50, 55, 56, 72, 53, 68, 69, 59, 60, 77, 78, 76, 75, 81, 79, 80, 83, 84, 95, 96, 49, 63, 62, 66, 89, 67, 92, 82, 91, 85, 86, 87, 88, 74?, 98?, 61, 93, 94, 101, 102, 65?, 104, 99, 100, 105, ?, 108, 97, 109, 110, 111, 106, 112, 113, 114.

Again, as in the case of Ibn Mas'ūd above this list is incomplete and does not contain all 114 *sūras* of the Qur'ān.

'Ubay has a total of 93 variants in *Sūra al-baqara*.[43] Very often, his readings are similar to those of Ibn Mas'ūd. For example, he reads *al-baqara* in 2: 70 as *al-baqira*. So does Ibn Mas'ūd.

The Muṣḥaf of Ibn 'Abbās (d. 68H/687)

Ibn 'Abbās also wrote a *muṣḥaf*, which according to the *Itqān*[44] also included the two additional *sūras* which Ubay had. Again his arrangement of the *sūras* differed from the other copies. In *Sūra al-baqara*, he has a total of 21 variants,

note 41 continued

and what was not part of the Qur'ān, when the revelation had ceased, and if e.g. this *ḥadīth* occurred in the *muṣḥaf* of Ubay, it was a *muṣḥaf* for his own personal use, in other words, his private notebook, where he did not always distinguish between Qur'ānic material and *ḥadīth*, since it was not meant for general use and he himself knew well what to make of his own notes. The same is true of the other copies of the Qur'ān, which some of the Companions had for their own personal use. Also those who transmitted to us the reports about these copies of the Qur'ān of the Companions have only narrated to us the various differences which occurred there according to reports that reached them (e.g. the *ḥadīth* in Bukhārī, VIII, No. 446 that Ubay at some early stage held this sentence to be part of the Qur'ān). However the actual manuscripts of these copies of the Qur'ān of the Companions have not come down to us, since all of them agreed on the correctness and validity of the copies which 'Uthmān had arranged to be written and distributed for general use. Hence their own personal notebooks became obsolete and were destroyed.

42 *Fihrist*, I, pp.58-60.

43 Again taken as example only to illustrate the point.

44 I, p.65; Ibn Abī Dawūd, *maṣāḥif*, p.193.

some of them identical with Ibn Mas'ūd and Ubay as well as other Companions.

Some other Companions

According to the *Itqān*[45] the *muṣḥaf* of Abū Mūsā al-Ash'arī (d.44H/664) contained the same material as Ubay had.

There is only one variant reported from him in *Sūra al-baqara*, namely that he read Ibraham in place of Ibrāhīm.

Ḥafṣa (d. 45H/665) had three variants in the same *sūra*, and Anas b. Mālik (d. 91H/709) had five.

Examples:

To further illustrate, here are a number of examples. They have been taken, as far as possible, from well-known *sūras*. While perhaps better examples exist to illustrate the points under discussion, they might not be understood as easily by readers less familiar with the Qur'ānic text.

Difference in vowelling:

Ibn 'Abbās[46] is reported to have read in *Sūra* 111:4:

ḥāmilatun al-ḥaṭab, in place of

ḥammālata-l-ḥaṭab

which could not be distinguished on the basis of the early written text, which omitted both *ḥaraka* and *alif*. The actual text must have looked something like this: حملت الحطب

Difference in spelling:

Ibn 'Abbās[47] reportedly wrote in *Sūra* 1:6 as well as all other places the word *al-ṣirāṭ* as *al-sirāṭ*.

Some variants attributed to Ibn Mas'ūd:[48]

1. in *Sūra al-fātiḥa*:

---

45 I, p.65; Ibn Abī Dāwūd, *maṣāhif*, p.210.
46 *ibid.*, p.208.
47 *ibid.*, p.195.
48 *ibid.*, p.25.

1:6	he read	*arshidnā*	in place of	*ihdinā*
	,, ,,	*man*	,, ,, ,,	*al-ladhīna*
	,, ,,	*ghaira*	,, ,, ,,	*ghairi*

2. in *Sūra al-baqara:*

2:2	he read	*tanzīlu-l-kitābi*	in place of	*dhālika-l-kitābu*
2:7	,, ,,	*ghishwatun*	,, ,, ,,	*ghishāwatun*
2:9	,, ,,	*yakhda'ūna*	,, ,, ,,	*yukhādi'ūna*
2:14	,, ,,	*bi-shayāṭīnihim*	,, ,, ,,	*ilā shayāṭīnihim* etc.

Variants on Sūra Al-Ikhlāṣ (112)

Verse	Ibn Mas'ūd[49]	'Ubaid[50]	'Umar[51]	normal reading by
112:1	*qul* omitted *al-wāḥid,* in place of *al-aḥad*	*qul* omitted	*qul* omitted	'Alī, Ibn 'Abbās, Abū Mūsā, Ḥafṣa, Anas b. Mālik, Zaid b. Thābit, Ibn Al-Zubair, Ibn 'Amr,
112:2	omitted			
112:3	*lam yulad wa lam yulid,* in place of *lam yalid wa lam yūlad*			'Ā'isha, Sālim, Umm Salama, 'Ubaid b. 'Umar

Even today the variants and synonyms are found in such copies of the text as are attributed to the Companions and are of some value to us in the sense that they may have served as an early rudimentary form of *tafsīr.* For example, according to

49 *ibid.*, p.113.
50 *ibid.*, p.180.
51 *ibid.*, p.222.

some reports the words *'ṣalāt al-wuṣṭā'* (middle prayer) were read and written by Ḥafṣa,[52] Ubay[53] and Ibn 'Abbās[54] as *'ṣalāt al-'aṣr'* (i.e. afternoon prayer).

As long as the *ṣaḥāba* wrote their own copies for personal use only, there was nothing wrong, if they did not strictly adhere to the order of *sūras* which was the order of the Qur'ān. Later on, when 'Uthmān's copy became the standard version, the Companions adopted the order of this copy including Ibn Mas'ūd who perhaps differed most.[55]

There were also, as indicated, some variant readings in these copies,[56] when some words were pronounced and spelt in slightly different ways, etc. However, it should be noted that variant readings are usually reported by a single person only, and occasionally by perhaps two or three while the version called the 'Uthmānic text is *mutawātir*, i.e. transmitted by numerous people and is without doubt authentic.

THE MUṢḤAF OF 'UTHMĀN

During the time of 'Uthmān differences in reading the Qur'ān became obvious, and after consultation with the Companions, 'Uthmān had a standard copy prepared from the *ṣuḥuf* of Abū Bakr that were kept with Ḥafṣa at that time.

The following is the report transmitted in the *Ṣaḥīḥ* Bukhārī:

> Narrated Anas bin Mālik: Ḥudhaifa bin Al-Yamān came to 'Uthmān at the time when the people of Shām and the people of Iraq were waging war to conquer Armīnya and Ādharbījān. Ḥudhaifa was afraid of their (the people of Shām and Iraq) differences in the recitation of the Qur'ān, so he said to 'Uthmān, 'O chief of the Believers! Save this nation before they differ about the Book

52 *Muwaṭṭa'* Mālik; Jeffery, p.214.
53 Jeffery, p.122.
54 Jeffery, p.196.
55 Ibn Abī Dāwūd, p.12; Ṣāliḥ, S.: *Mabāḥith fī 'ulūm al-qur'ān*, Beirut, 1964, p.83.
56 See also below, seven readings and *qira'āt*.

(Qur'ān), as Jews and the Christians did before'. So 'Uthmān sent a message to Ḥafṣa saying, 'Send us the manuscripts of the Qur'ān so that we may compile the Qur'ānic materials in perfect copies and return the manuscripts to you'. Ḥafṣa sent it to 'Uthmān. 'Uthmān then ordered Zaid bin Thābit, 'Abdullāh bin Az-Zubair, Sa'īd bin Al-'Āṣ and 'Abdur Raḥmān bin Ḥārith bin Hishām to rewrite the manuscripts in perfect copies. 'Uthmān said to the three Quraishī men, 'In case you disagree with Zaid bin Thābit on any point in the Qur'ān, then write it in the dialect of Quraish as the Qur'ān was revealed in their tongue'. They did so, and when they had written many copies, 'Uthmān returned the original manuscripts to Ḥafṣa. 'Uthmān sent to every Muslim province one copy of what they had copied, and ordered that all the other Qur'ānic materials whether written in fragmentary manuscripts or whole copies, be burnt. Zaid bin Thābit added, 'A verse from Sūra al-Aḥzāb was missed by me when we copied the Qur'ān and I used to hear Allah's Apostle reciting it. So we searched for it and found it with Khuzaima bin Thābit Al-Anṣārī'. (That verse was): 'Among the Believers are men who have been true in their convenant with Allah' (33:23).[57]

The following events led to the preparation of the *muṣḥaf* of 'Uthmān:

— Disputes had arisen among the Muslims about the correct manner of reciting the Qur'ān.
— 'Uthmān borrowed the *ṣuḥuf*, which were kept with Ḥafṣa.
— 'Uthmān ordered four Companions, among them Zaid bin Thābit, to rewrite the script in perfect copies.
— 'Uthmān sent these copies to the main centres of the Muslims to replace other materials that were in circulation.

57 Bukhārī, VI, No.510.

Chronology of the Written Text

Around 610	Muḥammad's prophethood commences.	1st revelation in cave on Mount Ḥirā'.	Transmitted orally, later in written form.
610–32	Muḥammad in Makka and Madina.	Continuous revelation on numerous occasions.	Transmitted orally, after memorisation by many, and writing down of revelation by various Companions upon the direct instruction of the Prophet himself.
632	Prophet's death.	Last revelation few days before this.	Complete revelation left behind both in the memories of various Companions as well as on various writing materials.
		At the death of the Prophet *complete* revelation left behind.	
632–34	Abū Bakr's caliphate.		
633	During the battle of Yamāma several Companions who knew the Qur'ān by heart were killed.	Abū Bakr instructs Zaid b. Thābit to prepare a single copy of the complete revelation.	Zaid b. Thābit brings together all the revelation into the *ṣuḥuf*, from both oral as well as written sources, demanding two

			witnesses for each piece. The *ṣuḥuf* remain with Abū Bakr.
		During the 1st/2nd year after the Prophet's death the entire revelation was copied onto sheets (*ṣuḥuf*).	
634–44	'Umar's caliphate.		The *ṣuḥuf* remain with 'Umar.
644–56	'Uthmān's caliphate.		The *ṣuḥuf* remain with Ḥafṣa bint 'Umar.
653	Campaign against Armenia and Azerbaidjan.	Serious differences arose among Muslims about the correct recitation of the Qur'ān. 'Uthmān instructs Zaid together with three other *ṣaḥāba* to prepare copies from the *ṣuḥuf* kept with Ḥafṣa.	Zaid and three Companions prepare a number of fresh copies from the *ṣuḥuf*. These copies are sent to the various Muslim regions to replace other material in circulation. *Ṣuḥuf* returned to Ḥafṣa. 'Uthmān also keeps one copy (*muṣḥaf*).
		Several copies of the entire revelation available throughout the Muslim lands.	

What the Prophet left to the Muslims

The revelation, as left by the Prophet, was available both orally and written on various materials. Its internal order was known to the Muslims and strictly observed by them.

Abū Bakr collected these loose materials and had their contents written on to sheets (*ṣuḥuf*).

The Difference between Abū Bakr's and 'Uthmān's Collection

Abū Bakr had made one single copy from the various verbal and written material. This copy was later kept by 'Umar and then by his daughter Ḥafṣa.

'Uthmān had many copies prepared from this copy and sent them to various places in the Muslim world, while the original *ṣuḥuf* were returned to Ḥafṣa and remained with her until her death. Later, Marwān b. Ḥakam (d. 65/684), according to a report in Ibn Abī Dāwūd, collected it from her heirs and had it destroyed, presumably fearing it might become the cause for new disputes. 'Uthmān also kept one of the copies for himself. This version of the text, also known as '*Muṣḥaf 'Uthmānī*' in fact constitutes the *ijmā'* (consensus) of the *ṣaḥāba*, all of whom agreed that it contained what Muḥammad had brought as revelation from Allah.[58]

The wide distribution of this text and its undisputed authority can also be deduced from the reports on the battle of Ṣiffīn (A.H. 37) 27 years after the death of the Prophet, and five years after 'Uthmān's copies were distributed, Mu'āwiya's troops fixed sheets from the Qur'ān on their spears to interrupt the battle.[59] However nobody accused anyone else of using a 'partisan' version of the text, which would have made a splendid accusation against the enemy.

---

58 According to Ibn Abī Dāwūd (117-8) eleven changes were made under al-Hajjāj, among them e.g. 5: 48 *'sharī'atan wa minhājan'* into *'shir'atan wa minhājan'*; 12: 45 *'anā ātīkum bi-ta'wīlihi'* into *anā unabbi'ukum bi-ta'wīlihi*. These are again according to Ibn Abī Dāwūd, mistakes which were made in the preparation of 'Uthmān's copy (pp.37-49). The first version of 12: 45 e.g. was the reading of 'Ubay (*ibid.*, p.138) and Ibn Mas'ūd (*ibid.*, p.39).

59 See Suyūṭī, *History of the Caliphs*, transl. H. S. Jarrett, Baptist Mission Press, Calcutta, 1881, p.177.

CHAPTER 3

The Qur'ān in Manuscript and Print

THE QUR'ĀNIC SCRIPT

Writing, although not very widespread in pre-Islamic time, was well-known among the Arabs. The script used in the seventh century, i.e. during the lifetime of the Prophet Muḥammad, consisted of very basic symbols, which expressed only the consonantal structure of a word, and even that with much ambiguity.

While today letters such as *bā, tā, thā, yā,* are easily distinguished by points, this was not so in the early days and all these letters used to be written simply as a straight line.

From this very basic system of writing there developed over the ages, various types of script, such as *Kūfī*, *Maghribī*, *Naskh*, etc., which spread all over the world.

The later invention of printing with standardised types has contributed to formalising the writing.

However, as far as the actual script of the Qur'ān is concerned, there were two important steps which brought about the forms in which we have the Qur'ānic text as it is today. These were the introduction of:

— Vowelling marks (*tashkīl*).
— Diacritical marks (*i'jām*).

Tashkīl

Tashkīl is the name for the signs indicating the vowels in Arabic scripts. They were apparently unknown in pre-Islamic times. These signs help to determine the correct pronunciation of the word and to avoid mistakes.

Example:

Byt بيت Baitun بَيْتٌ

When more and more Muslims of non-Arab origin and also many ignorant Arabs[1] studied the Qur'ān, faulty pronunciation and wrong readings began to increase. It is related that at the time of Du'alī (d. 69H/638) someone in Baṣra read the following *āya* from the Qur'ān in a faulty way, which changed the meaning completely: اَنَّ اللّٰهَ بَرِىٓءٌ مِنَ الْمُشْرِكِيْنَ وَرَسُوْلُهٗ

'That God and His apostle dissolve obligations with the pagans' (9: 3).

'That God dissolves obligations with the pagans and the apostle.' ان اللّٰه برىء من المشركين ورسوله

The mistake occurred through wrongly reading *rasūlihī* رَسُوْلِهٖ in place of *rasūluhū*, رَسُوْلُهٗ which could not be distinguished from the written text, because there were no signs or accents indicating the correct pronunciation. Unless someone had memorised the correct version he could out of ignorance easily commit such a mistake.[2] The signs or accents to prevent such problems were introduced not long before the *i'jām* and then got the shape they have to this day:[3]

Name	Old Style	New Style
Fatḥa	ب with dot above	بَ
Kasra	ب with dot below	بِ
Ḍamma	•ب	بُ

For an example of the old style see plate 5.

It has been suggested that the origin of *fatḥa* is *alif*, the origin of *kasra* is *yā* (without dots as in early books), and the origin of *ḍamma* is *wāw*. *Hamza* was previously written as 2 dots.[4]

---

1 Yaqūt reports in his book *irshād* that al-Ḥajjāj b. Yūsuf himself once read *aḥabba* in 9: 24 wrongly as *aḥabbu;* see GdQ, III, 124; note 6.

2 See also *fihrist*, I, pp. 87-8.

3 Hughes, T. P.: *A Dictionary of Islam*. London, 1895, p.687.

4 Abbott, N.: *The Rise of the North-Arabic Script and its Koranic Development*, Chicago, 1939, p.39.

I'jām (to provide a letter with a diacritical point)

The Arabic letters, as we know them today, are made up of lines and points. The latter are called *i'jām*. The ancient Arabic script did not have them, but consisted of strokes only.

The addition of diacritical points to the plain writing of strokes helped to distinguish the various letters which could be easily mixed up.

Example: ٮٮٮ بيت

Without dots this word cannot be easily recognised. With *i'jām*, the letters of this word can easily be distinguished.

Although the *i'jām* (diacritical points) were already known in pre-Islamic times, they were rarely used. The very early copies of the Qur'ānic manuscripts (and Arabic writing in general) did not have these signs. They were apparently introduced into the Qur'ānic script during the time of the fifth Umayyad Caliph, 'Abd al-Malik bin Marwān (66-86H/685-705) and the governorship of Al-Ḥajjāj in Iraq, when more and more Muslims began to read and study the Qur'ān, some of whom did not know much of the Qur'ān, and others were of non-Arab origin. It is said of the well-known *tābi'ī* Al-Du'alī that he was the first to introduce these points into the Qur'ānic text.

EARLY MANUSCRIPTS

Writing Material

Early manuscripts of the Qur'ān were typically written on animal skin. We know that in the lifetime of the Prophet, parts of the revelation were written on all kinds of materials, such as bone, animal skin, palm risps, etc. The ink was prepared from soot.

Script

All old Qur'ānic script is completely without any diacritical points or vowel signs as explained above. Also there are no headings or separations between the *sūras* nor any other kind of division, nor even any formal indication of the end of a verse. Scholars distinguish between two types of early writing:

— *Kūfī*, which is fairly heavy and not very dense.
— *Ḥijāzī*, which is lighter, more dense and slightly inclined towards the right.

Some believe that the *Ḥijāzī* is older than the *Kūfī*, while others say that both were in use at the same time, but that *Ḥijāzī* was the less formal style.[5]

Some Peculiarities of the Ancient Writing

Numerous copies of the Qur'ān were made after the time of the Prophet Muḥammad and the Rightly-Guided Caliphs, and the writers of these manuscripts strictly observed the autography of the 'Uthmānic Qur'ān. There are, compared to the usual Arabic spelling, some peculiarities. Here are a few of them, only concerning the letters *alif*, *yā*, *wāw*, by way of examples:[6]

— The letter *alif* is often written on top of a letter instead of after it, e.g. رَبِّ الْعٰلَمِينَ,
— The letter *yā* (or *alif*) of the word is omitted, e.g.: النَّبِيّٖنَ
— Some words have the letter *wāw* in place of *alif*, e.g.: الصَّلٰوةَ

OLD MANUSCRIPTS OF THE QUR'ĀN

Most of the early original Qur'ān manuscripts, complete or in sizeable fragments, that are still available to us now, are not

5 This is the view of N. Abbott: 'We can no longer draw a chronological demarcation line between what are commonly termed the Kufī and the Naskhī scripts, nor can we consider the latter as a development of the former. This . . . now demands a more general recognition. Our materials show that there were two tendencies at work simultaneously, both of them natural ones' (Abbott, *op. cit.*, p.16). See plates 5 and 6.

6 For more examples see Kamāl, *op. cit.*, pp.47-9; a list of these peculiarities has been provided by M. Ḥamidullah: 'Orthographical Peculiarities in the text of the Qur'ān', in: *Islamic Order*, 3 (4), 1981, pp.72-86.

earlier than the second century after the *Hijra*. The earliest copy, which was exhibited in the British Museum during the 1976 World of Islam Festival, dated from the late second century.[7] However, there are also a number of odd fragments of Qur'ānic papyri available, which date from the first century.[8]

There is a copy of the Qur'ān in the Egyptian National Library on parchment made from gazelle skin, which has been dated 68 *Hijra* (688 A.D.), i.e. 58 years after the Prophet's death.

What happened to 'Uthmān's Copies?

It is not known exactly how many copies of the Qur'ān were made at the time of 'Uthmān, but Suyūṭī[9] says: 'The well-known ones are five'. This probably excludes the copy that 'Uthmān kept for himself. The cities of Makka, Damascus, Kufa, Basra and Madina each received a copy.[10]

There are a number of references in the older Arabic literature on this topic which together with latest information available may be summarised as follows:

The Damascus Manuscript

Al-Kindī (d. around 236/850) wrote in the early third century that three out of four of the copies prepared for 'Uthmān were destroyed in fire and war, while the copy sent to Damascus was still kept at his time at Malatja.[11]

Ibn Baṭūṭa (779/1377) says he has seen copies or sheets from the copies of the Qur'ān prepared under 'Uthmān in Granada, Marakesh, Basra and other cities.[12]

Ibn Kathīr (d. 774/1372) relates that he has seen a copy of

---

7 Lings, M. and Y. H. Safadi: *The Qur'ān*, London, 1976, No. 1A. See also plate 6.

8 Grohmann, A.: 'Die Entstehung des Koran und die ältesten Koran-Handschriften', in: *Bustan*, 1961, pp.33-8.

9 Makhdūm, I.: *Tarīkh al-muṣḥaf al-'Uthmānī fī Ṭāshqand,* Tashkent 1391/1971, p.17.

10 GdQ, III, 6, Note 1.

11 GdQ, III, 6, Note 1.

12 *Ṣāliḥ*, *op. cit.*, p.87.

the Qur'ān attributed to 'Uthmān, which was brought to Damascus in the year 518 *Hijra* from Tiberias (Palestine). He said it was 'very large, in beautiful clear strong writing with strong ink, in parchment, I think, made of camel skin'.[13]

Some believe that the copy later on went to Leningrad and from there to England. After that nothing is known about it. Others hold that this *muṣḥaf* remained in the mosque of Damascus, where it was last seen before the fire in the year 1310/1892.[14]

The Egyptian Manuscript

There is a copy of an old Qur'ān kept in the mosque of al-Ḥussain in Cairo. Its script is of the old style, although *Kūfī*, and it is quite possible that it was copied from the *Muṣḥaf* of 'Uthmān.[15]

The Madīna Manuscript

Ibn Jubair (d. 614/1217) saw the manuscript in the mosque of Madīna in the year 580/1184. Some say it remained in Madīna until the Turks took it from there in 1334/1915. It has been reported that this copy was removed by the Turkish authorities to Istanbul, from where it came to Berlin during World War I. The Treaty of Versailles, which concluded World War I, contains the following clause:

> 'Article 246: Within six months from the coming into force of the present Treaty, Germany will restore to His Majesty, King of Hedjaz, the original Koran of Caliph Othman, which was removed from Medina by the Turkish authorities and is stated to have been presented to the ex-Emperor William II.'[16]

---

13 *ibid.*, p.88.

14 *ibid.*, p.89; Muir, in 'The Mameluke Dynasties' also writes that this manuscript was burnt in Damascus in 1893; see Abbott, *op. cit.*, p.51.

15 Kamāl, *op. cit.*, p.56.

16 Israel, Fred L. (ed.): *Major Peace Treaties of Modern History*, New York, Chelsea House Pub., Vol.II, p.1418.

The manuscript then reached Istanbul, but not Madīna.[17]

The 'Imām' Manuscript

This is the name used for the copy which 'Uthmān kept himself, and it is said he was killed while reading it.[18]

According to some the Umayyads took it to Andalusia, from where it came to Fās (Morocco) and according to Ibn Baṭūṭa it was there in the eighth century after the *Hijra,* and there were traces of blood on it. From Morocco, it might have found its way to Samarkand.

The Samarkand Manuscript[19]

This is the copy now kept in Tashkent (Uzbekistan). It may be the *Imām* manuscript or one of the other copies made at the time of 'Uthmān.

It came to Samarkand in 890 *Hijra* (1485) and remained there till 1868. Then it was taken to St. Petersburg by the Russians in 1869. It remained there till 1917. A Russian orientalist gave a detailed description of it, saying that many pages were damaged and some were missing. A facsimile, some 50 copies, of this *muṣḥaf* was produced by S. Pisareff in 1905. A copy was sent to the Ottoman Sultan 'Abdul Ḥamid, to the *Shāh* of Iran, to the *Amīr* of Bukhara, to Afghanistan, to Fās and some important Muslim personalities. One copy is now in the Columbia University Library (U.S.A.).[20]

The manuscript was afterwards returned to its former place and reached Tashkent in 1924, where it has remained since. Apparently the Soviet authorities have made further copies, which are presented from time to time to visiting Muslim

---

17 The same information about this copy was published in a Cairo magazine in 1938 (*Makhdūm, op. cit.*, p.19). Surprisingly the standard book *Geschichte des Qorans*, the third part of which was published in Germany in 1938, i.e. well after the Treaty of Versailles, although discussing the 'Uthmānic Qur'ān and old manuscripts in detail, makes no reference whatsoever to this event. Also, the writer of the *History of the Muṣḥaf of 'Uthmān in Tashkent*, indicates that he does not know what to make of this reference.

18 Ibn Sa'd: *al-ṭabaqāt al-kubrā*, Cairo, n.d., Vol. III, (1), pp. 51-2.

19 *Makhdūm, op. cit.*, p.22ff.

20 *The Muslim World*, Vol. 30 (1940), pp.357-8.

heads of state and other important personalities. In 1980, photocopies of such a facsimile were produced in the United States, with a two-page foreword by M. Hamidullah.

The writer of the *History of the Muṣḥaf of 'Uthmān in Tashkent* gives a number of reasons for the authenticity of the manuscript. They are, excluding the various historical reports which suggest this, as follows:

— The fact that the *muṣḥaf* is written in a script used in the first half of the first century *Hijra*.
— The fact that it is written on parchment from a gazelle, while later Qur'āns are written on paper-like sheets.
— The fact that it does not have any diacritical marks which were introduced around the eighth decade of the first century; hence the manuscript must have been written before that.
— The fact that it does not have the vowelling symbols introduced by Du'alī, who died in 68 *Hijra*; hence it is earlier than this.

In other words: two of the copies of the Qur'ān which were originally prepared in the time of Caliph 'Uthmān, are still available to us today and their text and arrangement can be compared, by anyone who cares to, with any other copy of the Qur'ān, be it in print or handwriting, from any place or period of time. They will be found identical.

The 'Alī Manuscript

Some sources indicate that a copy of the Qur'ān written by the fourth Caliph 'Alī is kept in Najaf, Iraq, in the Dār al-Kutub al-'Alawiya. It is written in *Kūfī* script, and on it is written: "Alī bin Abī Ṭālib wrote it in the year 40 of the *Hijra*'.[21]

---

21 Aṭṭar, D.: *Mūjaz 'ulūm al-qur'ān*, Beirut 1399/1979, p.116.

From the sixteenth century, when the printing press with movable type was first used in Europe and later in all parts of the world, the pattern of writing and of printing the Qur'ān was further standardised.

There were already printed copies of the Qur'ān before this, in the so-called block-print form, and some specimens from as early as the tenth century, both of the actual wooden blocks and the printed sheets, have come down to us.[22]

The first extant Qur'ān for which movable type was used was printed in Hamburg (Germany) in 1694. The text is fully vocalised.[23] Probably the first Qur'ān printed by Muslims is the so-called 'Mulay Usman edition' of 1787, published in St. Petersburg, Russia, followed by others in Kazan (1828), Persia (1833) and Istanbul (1877).[24]

In 1858, the German orientalist Fluegel produced together with a useful concordance the so-called 'Fluegel edition' of the Qur'ān, printed in Arabic, which has since been used by generations of orientalists.[25] The Fluegel edition has however a very basic defect: its system of verse numbering is not in accordance with general usage in the Muslim world.[26]

The Egyptian Edition

The Qur'ānic text in printed form now used widely in the Muslim world and developing into a 'standard version', is the so-called 'Egyptian' edition, also known as the King Fu'ād edition, since it was introduced in Egypt under King Fu'ād. This edition is based on the reading of Ḥafṣ, as reported by 'Āṣim, and was first printed in Cairo in 1925/1344H. Numerous copies have since been printed.

---

22 Grohmann, *op. cit.*, p.38; Exhibition in the British Library, London.

23 Al-Coranus, lex islamitica Muhammedis, Officina Schultzio-Schilleriania, Hamburg, 1694; Exhibition No. 22.

24 Blachère, R.: *Introduction au Coran*, Paris, 1947, p.133.

25 Fluegel, Gustav: *Corani texti Arabicus.* Leipzig, 1834.

26 See e.g. 74:31, where he makes four verses out of one.

The Sa'īd Nursi Copy

Finally, the Qur'ān printed by the followers of Sa'īd Nursi from Turkey should be mentioned as an example of combining a hand-written beautifully illuminated text with modern offset printing technology. The text was hand written by the Turkish calligrapher Ḥāmid al-'Amidī. It was first printed in Istanbul in 1947, but since 1976 has been produced in large numbers and various sizes at the printing press run by the followers of Sa'īd Nursi in West Berlin (Germany).

CHAPTER 4

Form, Language and Style

DIVISIONS OF THE TEXT

Āya and Sūra

Āya (pl. *āyāt*) actually means 'sign'. In technical language it is the shortest division of the Qur'ānic text, i.e. a phrase or sentence. The revelation is guidance from God to mankind and it is therefore not at all surprising to find that its smallest divisions are called (guiding) 'signs'. The term 'verse' is not appropriate since the Qur'ān is not poetry.

Sūra (pl. *Suwar*) means literally 'row' or 'fence'. In technical language, it is the passage-wise division of the Qur'ānic text, i.e. a chapter or part, set apart from the preceding and following text.

The Qur'ān has 114 *sūras* of unequal length, the shortest consisting of four and the longest of 286 *āyāt*.

All *sūras* (with the exception of *Sūra* 9) begin with the words *bismillāhir raḥmānir raḥīm*. This is not a later addition to the text, but was already used, even before Muḥammad's call to prophethood.[1]

All 114 *sūras* in the Qur'ān have names, which serve as a sort of heading. The names are often derived from an important or distinguishing word in the text itself, such as e.g. *al-anfāl* (8) or *al-baqara* (2). In other cases it is one of the first few words with which the *sūra* begins e.g. *ṭā-hā* (20) or *al-furqān* (25).

1 See *Sūra* 27:30.

Order and Arrangement

Both the order of the *āyāt* within each *sūra* and the arrangement of the *sūras* were finally determined by the Prophet under guidance from the Angel Gabriel in the year of his death, when Gabriel twice came to revise the text with him.[2]

Scholars have also grouped the *sūras* into four kinds:

1 *al-ṭiwāl* (long ones): 2-10.

2 *al-mi'ūn: sūras* with approximately 100 *ayāt*: 10-35.

3 *al-mathānī*: *sūras* with less than 100 *ayāt*: 36-49.

4 *al-mufaṣṣal*: the last section of the Qur'ān beginning with *Sūra qāf*: 50-114.

Other Divisions of the Text

Juz' (pl. *ajzā'*) literally means part, portion. The Qur'ān is divided into 30 portions of approximately equal length for easy recitation during the thirty nights of a month, especially of the month of Ramaḍān. Usually they are indicated by the word and the number of it given alongside, (e.g. جزء *juz'* 30 beginning with *Sūra* 78).

Some copies of the Qur'ān have the *sūras* divided into paragraphs called *rukū'*. They are indicated by the symbol ع and the explanation of the Arabic numerals written with each is as follows, e.g. 2: 20:

— The top figure (2) indicates that this is the second completed *rukū'* in the respective *sūra* (here *Sūra al-baqara*).

— The middle figure (13) indicates that this completed *rukū'* contains 13 *āyāt*.

— The lower figure (2) indicates that this is the second *rukū'* in the respective *juz'* (here first *juz'*).

Copies of the Qur'ān printed in the Middle East in particular have each *juz'* subdivided into four *ḥizb* indicated by the sign حزب e.g. 2: 74 is the beginning of the second *ḥizb* of the

---

2 See above, transmission of the Qur'ānic revelation, p. 31.

Qur'ān, indicated by the figure 2: حزب ٢

Each *ḥizb* is again subdivided into quarters, indicated as follows:

— First quarter of the *ḥizb*: ربع الحزب

— Half of the *ḥizb*: نصف الحزب

— Third quarter of the *ḥizb*: ثلاثة ارباع الحزب

The Qur'ānic text is also divided into seven parts of approximately equal length, called *manzil*, for recitation over seven days, indicated in some copies by the word *manzil* منزل and the respective number in the margin. The following table shows the division of the text into *juz'* and *manzil*:[3]

Manzil	*Juz'*	*Sūra*
1	1	1:1
	2	2:142
	3	2:253
	4	3:92 or 93
	5	4:24
	6	4:148
2	6	5:1
	7	5:82 or 83
	8	6:111
	9	7:88
	9	7:286
	10	8:41
	11	9:93 or 94
3	11	10:1
	12	11:6
	13	12:53
	13	13:15

3 Hamidullah, Muhammad: *Le Saint Coran. Traduction integrale et notes*, Paris: Club Francais du Livre, n.d., p.XLI.

	14	15: 1 or 2
	14	16: 50
4	15	17: 1
	15	17: 109
	16	18: 75
	16	19: 58
	17	21: 1
	17	22: 18
	17	22: 77
	18	23: 1
	19	25: 21
	19	25: 60
5	19	27: 1
	19	27: 26
	20	27: 56 or 60
	21	29: 45 or 46
	21	32: 15
	22	33: 31
6	22	35: 1
	23	36: 22 or 28
	23	38: 24 or 25
	24	39: 32
	24	41: 38
	25	41: 47
	26	46: 1
7	26	50: 1
	27	51: 31
	27	53: 62
	28	58: 1
	29	67: 1
	30	78: 1
	30	84: 21
	30	96: 19

The ends of the various *manzil* according to Qatāda are 4: 76; 8: 36; 15: 49; 23: 118; 34: 54; 49: 18 and 114: 6.[4]

4 Ibn Abī Dawūd, p.118.

LANGUAGE AND VOCABULARY

The language of the Qur'ān – as is well known – is Arabic. The Qur'ān itself gives some indication about its language:

> 'We have sent it down as an Arabic Qur'ān in order that ye may learn wisdom' (12: 2).

In another place the language of the Qur'ān is called 'pure Arabic' (*'arabiyyun mubīn*):

> 'This (tongue) is Arabic, pure and clear' (16: 103).

The question that arises is: Why was the Qur'ān revealed in Arabic, and not in any other language? The first and perhaps the most obvious reason is already referred to in the Qur'ān, namely that because the messenger who was to announce this message was an Arab, it is only natural that the message should be announced in his language:

> 'Had We sent this as a Qur'ān (in a language) other than Arabic they could have said: Why are not its verses explained in detail? What! (a book) not in Arabic and (a messenger) an Arab? Say: It is a guide and a healing to those who believe . . .' (41: 44).

Another important reason concerns the audience which was to receive the message. The message had to be in a language understood by the audience to whom it was first addressed, i.e. the inhabitants of Makka and the surrounding areas:

> 'Thus We have sent by inspiration to thee an Arabic Qur'ān: that thou mayest warn the mother of the cities and all around her – and warn (them) of the day of assembly of which there is no doubt (when) some will be in the garden and some in the blazing fire' (42: 7).

The Qur'ān Needed to be Understood

The Qur'ān contains revelation from Allah and the true

nature of revelation is to guide mankind from darkness to light:

> 'A book which we have revealed unto thee in order that thou mightest lead mankind out of the depths of darkness into light – by the leave of thy Lord – to the way of (Him) the exalted in power, worthy of all praise' (14: 1).

The revelation came in the language of the messenger and his people in order that it might be understood:

> 'We have made it a Qur'ān in Arabic that ye may be able to understand (and learn wisdom)' (43: 3).

In the process of understanding a message two steps are essential:

— To receive the message correctly and completely, in this case to receive its words correctly and completely.
— To 'decode' it, to grasp the meanings of the message received.

Only the combination of the two elements, i.e. reception and decoding, lead to proper understanding of the message.

To Understand the Qur'ān

It is not correct to assume that understanding the Qur'ān in order to take guidance from it depends upon direct knowledge of the Arabic language, since there are numerous Arabic-speaking people who do not understand the message of the Qur'ān. Rather the Qur'ān tells us that right guidance comes only from Allah:

> 'This is the guidance of God: He giveth that guidance to whom He pleaseth of His worshippers. . .' (6: 88).

However, to understand the language of the Qur'ān is a prerequisite to fully grasp its meanings. Hence many Muslims have learned this language. Others, who have not done so, make use of translations, which for them is an indirect means of knowing the language, as in the translations the meanings of the Qur'ān have been rendered into their mother tongues so that they may familiarise themselves with the message from Allah.

This message can be understood by all human beings who are willing to listen, for the Qur'ān is not difficult but easy:

> 'We have indeed made the Qur'ān easy to remember: but is there any that remembers it?' (54: 17).

Non-Arabic Words in the Qur'ān

There is some difference of opinion among scholars whether the language of the Qur'ān includes expressions which are not Arabic. Some (among them Ṭabarī and Bāqillānī) hold that all in the Qur'ān is Arabic and that words of non-Arabic origin found in the Qur'ān were nevertheless part of Arabic speech. Although these words were of non-Arab origin the Arabs used and observed them and they became genuinely integrated in the Arabic language.

However, it is conceded that there are non-Arabic proper names in the Qur'ān, such as Isrā'īl, Imrān, Nūḥ, etc.

Others have said that the Qur'ān does contain words not used in the Arabic language, such as e.g.:

— al-Qisṭās (17:35), derived from the Greek language.
— al-Sijjīl (15: 74), derived from the Persian language.
— al-Ghassāq (78: 25), derived from the Turkish language.
— al-Ṭūr (2:63), derived from the Syriac language.
— al-Kifl (57: 28), derived from the Abyssinian language.

Some scholars have written books on the topic of 'foreign vocabulary in the Qur'ān', e.g. Suyūṭī, who compiled a small book with a list of 118 expressions in different languages.[5]

---

5 The *Mutawakkilī* of Al-Suyūṭī, trans. by William Y. Bell, Yale University Dissertations, 1924; see also *Itqān*.

LITERARY FORMS AND STYLE

The Qur'ān is the revelation from Allah for the guidance of mankind and not poetry or literature. Nevertheless it is expressed verbally and in written form, and hence its literary forms and style may be considered here briefly.

Broadly speaking there are two main literary forms:

— Prose.
— Poetry.

By prose is meant a way of expression close to the everyday spoken language, and distinct from poetry insofar as it lacks any conspicuous artifice of rhythm and rhyme.

The Qur'ān is not Poetry

Not only European orientalists have described some passages of the Qur'ān as more 'poetic' than others: the opponents of Muḥammad had already used this argument, accusing him of being a poet or a soothsayer. This is refuted by the Qur'ān itself:

> 'It is not the word of a poet; little it is ye believe! Nor is it the word of a soothsayer: little admonition it is ye receive. (This is) a message sent down from the Lord of the worlds' (69: 40-3).

The accusations against Muḥammad refuted in the above passage are based on the usage of a particular style, employed in the Qur'ān, which is said to be like *saj'* or close to it.

The word *saj'* is usually translated as 'rhymed prose', i.e. a literary form with some emphasis on rhythm and rhyme, but distinct from poetry. *Saj'* is not really as sophisticated as poetry, but has been employed by Arab poets, and is the best known of the pre-Islamic Arab prosodies. It is distinct from poetry in its lack of metre, i.e. it has no consistent rhythmic pattern, and it shares with poetry the element of rhyme,[6] though in many cases somewhat irregularly employed.

---

6 Called *fāṣila* (pl. *fawāṣil*) when used for the Qur'ān.

The Difference between Literature and the Qur'ān

Ibn Khaldūn (d. 809H/1406), the well-known author of the *muqaddima* pointed out in a passage on the literature of the Arabs the difference between literature and the Qur'ān in general and between *saj'* and the Qur'ān in particular:

> 'It should be known that the Arabic language and Arab speech are divided into two branches. One of them is rhymed poetry . . . The other branch is prose, that is, non-metrical speech . . . The Qur'ān is in prose. However, it does not belong in either of the two categories. It can neither be called straight prose nor rhymed prose. It is divided into verses. One reaches breaks where taste tells one that the speech stops. It is then resumed and "repeated" in the next verse. (Rhyme) letters, which would make that (type of speech) rhymed prose are not obligatory, nor do rhymes (as used in poetry) occur. This situation is what is meant by the verse of the Qur'ān:
>
> 'God revealed the best story, a book harmoniously arranged with repeated verses . . .' (39: 23).[7]

Examples:

A good example for a *saj'*-like passage in the Qur'ān would be *Sūra al-ikhlāṣ* (112: 1-4). It is somewhat irregular in its rhythm, and it has a rhyme ending with the syllable *ad*:

Qul huwa llāhu aḥad	Say: He is God the One and Only
Allāhus ṣamad	God the Eternal, Absolute
Lam yalid wa lam yūlad	He begetteth not nor is He begotten
wa lam yakun lahu kufuwan aḥad	And there is none like unto Him.

Of the many passages more like plain prose, although not quite identical to it, as the kind of end-rhyme indicates, the following may serve as an example:

---

7 Ibn Khaldun: *The Muqaddima*, Princeton, 1967, Vol. 3, p.368; Ibn Khaldun: *Muqaddima*, Cairo, n.d., p.424.

'Innā auḥainā ilaika kamā auḥainā ilā nūḥin wa nabiyīna min ba'dihī wa auḥainā ilā ibrāhīma wa ismā'īla wa isḥāqa wa ya'qūba wa-l-asbāṭi wa 'īsā wa ayyūba wa yūnusa wa ḥārūna wa sulaimāna wa ātainā dāwūda zabūra. Wa rusulan qad qaṣaṣnāhum 'alaika min qablu wa rusulan lam naqṣuṣhum 'alaika wa kallama llāhu mūsā taklīmā. Rusulan mubashshirīna wa mundhirīna li'allā yakūna li-nnāsi 'alā llāhi hujjatun ba'dar rusuli wa kāna llāhu 'azīzan ḥakīma (4: 163-5).	We have sent thee inspiration as We sent it to Noah and the messengers after him: We sent inspiration to Abraham, Ismail, Isaac, Jacob and the tribes, to Jesus, Job, Jonah, Aaron, and Solomon, and to David We gave the psalms. Of some apostles We have already told thee the story, of others We have not. And to Moses God spoke direct. Apostles who gave good news as well as warning that mankind after (the coming) of the apostles should have no plea against God: for God is exalted in power, wise.

STYLE

Narrative in the Qur'ān

The Qur'ān contains many narratives (*qiṣaṣ*, sg. *qiṣṣa*), referred to in the Qur'ān itself:

> 'We do relate unto thee the most beautiful of stories, in that We reveal to thee this (portion of the) Qur'ān. . .' (12: 3).

These narratives, which illustrate and underline important aspects of the Qur'ānic message, fulfil their functions in a variety of ways. The following are some of the more common patterns:

— Explanation of the general message of Islam.
— General guidance and reminder.
— Strengthening the conviction of the Prophet and the believers.
— Reminder of the earlier prophets and their struggle.

— Indication for the continuity and truth of Muḥammad's message.
— Providing arguments against some opponents of Islam, such as e.g. Jews and Christians.

As far as the contents of these narratives are concerned, one may, broadly speaking, distinguish between the following three kinds:

— Stories of the Prophets of Allah, their peoples, their message, their call, their persecution, etc.; such as e.g. the narratives about Nūḥ (*Sūra* 26), Mūsā (*Sūra* 28), 'Īsā (*Sūra* 19) and many others.
— Other Qur'ānic narratives about past people or events, such as the narratives about the Companions of the cave, or about Dhu-l-qarnain (*Sūra* 18).
— References to events that took place during the lifetime of the Prophet Muḥammad, such as the battle of Badr (3: 13), the battle of Uḥud (3: 121-8), the battle of Aḥzāb (33: 9-27), the *isrā'* (17: 1), etc.

Similes in the Qur'ān

The Qur'ān also employs similes (*amthāl,* sg. *mathal*) in many places to explain certain truths or to drive home important points of the message, by likening it to something well known or describing it in a pictorial manner.[8]

Example:

> 'He sends down water from the skies and the channels flow, each according to its measure; but the torrents bear away the foam that mounts up to the surface. Even so, from that (ore) which they heat in the fire to make ornaments or utensils therewith there is scum likewise, thus doth God (by parable) show forth the truth and vanity, for the scum disappears like froth cast out; while that which is for the good of mankind remains on the earth. Thus doth God set forth parables' (13: 17).

8 See, e.g. 16: 75-6.

Passages with Qul

More than 200 passages in the Qur'ān open with the word '*Qul*' (say:), which is an instruction to the Prophet Muḥammad to address the words following this introduction to his audience in a particular situation, such as e.g. in reply to a question that has been raised, or as an assertion of a matter of belief, or announcement of a legal ruling, etc.

Examples:

> 'Say: Nothing will happen to us except what God has decreed for us: He is our Protector. . .' (9: 51).
>
> 'Say: O people of the book. Do ye disapprove of us for no other reason than that we believe in God, and the revelation that has come to us and that which has come before (us) and perhaps that most of you are rebellious and disobedient?' (5: 62).
>
> 'They ask thee concerning (things taken as) spoils of war. Say: (Such) spoils are at the disposal of God and the apostle: for fear God and keep straight the relation between yourselves: obey God and His apostle, if ye do believe' (8: 1).

Oaths in the Qur'ān

In a number of places the Qur'ān employs oath-like expressions (*aqsām*, sg. *qasam*).[9] Their function is to strengthen and support an argument, and to disperse doubts in the mind of the listener. In the Arabic text these passages are often opened by the word '*wa*' or the phrase '*lā uqsimu*' (indeed I swear).

Examples:

Sometimes an oath is taken by Allah himself:

> 'But no, *by thy Lord*, they can have no real faith until they make thee judge in all disputes between them and

9 For a brief discussion see also Abdullah Yusuf Ali, *op. cit.*, App. XIV, pp. 1784-7.

find in their souls no resistance against thy decisions but accept them with fullest conviction' (4: 65).

Other oaths are taken by Allah's creation:

> '*By* the sun and his (glorious) splendour, *by* the moon as she follows him, *by* the day as it shows up (the sun's) glory, *by* the night as it conceals it; *by* the firmament and its (wonderful) structure, *by* the earth and its (wide) expanse, *by* the soul and the proportion and order given to it. . .' (91: 1-7).
>
> 'I do call to witness this city. . .' (90: 1).

Man should only take an oath by Allah, the creator, but not by anything created.

MUḤKAMĀT AND MUTASHĀBIHĀT

The word *muḥkamāt* (sg. *muḥkama*) is derived from the root *uḥkima* which means to decide between two things. It is a verbal noun in the plural, meaning judgements, decisions and in technical language refers to all clearly decided verses of the Qur'ān, mostly those concerning legal rulings, but also to other clear definitions such as between truth and falsehood etc. This is what is meant by 'general *muḥkamāt*'.

Mutashābihāt (sg. *mutashābiha*) is derived from the root *'ishtabaha'* meaning 'to be doubtful'. It is a verbal noun in the plural, meaning the uncertain or doubtful things. In technical language it refers to those verses of the Qur'ān the meanings of which are not clear or not completely agreed upon, but open to two or more interpretations.

Example of *muḥkamāt*:

> 'O you who believe! When ye deal with each other, in transactions involving future obligations, in a fixed period of time, reduce them to writing. Let a scribe write down faithfully as between the parties. . .' (2: 282).

Example of *mutashābihāt*:

> '(God) Most Gracious is firmly established on the throne (of authority)' (20: 5).

Note that the words in brackets have been added by the translator in an attempt to interpret this *āya*.

The Qur'ān on Muḥkamāt and Mutashābihāt

The Qur'ān says of itself that it contains two kinds of *āyāt*, both of which are fundamental components of the book, and both of which must be accepted:

> 'He it is who has sent down to thee the Book: in it are verses basic or fundamental (of established meaning); they are the foundation of the book: others are allegorical, that is those in whose hearts is perversity follow the part thereof that is allegorical, seeking discord and searching for its hidden meanings, but no one knows its hidden meanings except God and those who are firmly grounded in knowledge say: "We believe in the book; the whole of it is from our Lord;" and none will grasp the message except men of understanding' (3: 7).

Here *muḥkamāt* and *mutashābihāt* are described as follows:

muḥkama:
- Something of which knowledge was desired.
- Something with only one dimension.
- Something sufficient in meaning, requiring no further explanation.

mutashābihāt:
- Something known to Allah only.
- Something with more than one dimension.
- Something requiring further explanation.

Hence in the Qur'ān those *āyāt* dealing with *ḥalāl* and *ḥarām*, punishments, inheritance, promise and threat, etc.

belong to the *muḥkamāt*, while those concerning the attributes of Allah, the true nature of the resurrection, judgement and life after death etc. belong to the *mutashābihāt*.

General and Specific

Some verses of the Qur'ān are of a very wide, general application (*al-'ām*), e.g. including all human beings, or all Muslims etc. Other *ayāt* are restricted in their application to certain special circumstances only (*al-khāṣ*).

Example:

> 'Every soul shall have a taste of death' (3: 185)
>
> 'Let there be no obscenity, nor wickedness nor wrangling in the Hajj' (2: 187).
>
> 'God (thus) directs you as regards your children (inheritance)' (4: 11).

Furthermore one also distinguishes between 'general verses' which remain general, and others which intend a specific meaning.

Example:

> 'Pilgrimage thereto is a duty man owes to God – those who can afford the journey' (3: 97).

Of the 'special meanings' there are several varieties. Usually some kind of condition or limitation is specified.

Example:

> 'Your step-daughters under your guardianship, born of your wives *to whom you have gone in*' (4: 23).
>
> 'It is prescribed when death approaches any one of you, *if you leave any goods* that he make a bequest to parents and next of kin' (2: 180).
>
> 'So keep away from the women in their courses, and do not approach them *until* they are clean' (2: 222).

‘Free’ and ‘Bound’ Verses

Some of the *aḥkām* verses are valid, ‘free’ (*muṭlaq*) from any conditions or circumstances, while others are ‘bound’ *(muqayyad)* to special conditions or situations, and apply only therein.

Examples:

> ‘If it is beyond your means, fast for three days, that is expiation for the wrath ye have sworn’ (5: 92).

It is free, i.e. left to one’s discretion whether to fast three days consecutively or with interruptions.

> ‘And if ye find no water then take yourselves clean sand or earth and rub therewith your faces and hands’ (5: 6).[10]

‘Literal’ and ‘Understood’ Meanings

The meaning of certain *āyāt* is derived from the literal wording (*manṭūq*) while that of others is derived from what is understood (*mafhūm*) by them:

Of the literal understanding there are several kinds. The first concerns a clear text, i.e. a text clear and without ambiguity.

Example:

> ‘But if he cannot afford it, he should fast three days during the Hajj and seven days on his return, making ten days in all’ (2: 196).

In other cases the text may be somewhat ambiguous in its expression but obvious as far as the meaning is concerned.

Example:

> ‘And do not approach them until they are clean’ (2: 222).

The Arabic word *taṭahharna* may refer to the end of the

---

10 Some say this *āya* is ‘bound’, as the same *āya* mentioning *wuḍū’* instructs washing of the hands ‘to the elbows’; others say it is ‘free’.

woman's menstrual period, or the completion of the bath after the period; the second being more obvious.[11]

Still other verses imply a meaning through the context, although the wording itself is not clear.

Example:

> 'And out of kindness reward to them the wing of humility' (17:24).

This applies to parents, and not to all human beings in general, as the context of this verse suggests.

Al Muqaṭṭa'āt

The so-called 'abbreviated letters' are an important section of the *mutashābihāt*[12] insofar as their meanings are not known. The word is derived from the root '*qaṭa'a*' – to cut, and means 'what is cut', and also 'what is abbreviated'.

In technical language the word is used for certain letters found at the beginning of several *sūras* of the Qur'ān, called 'the abbreviated letters'.

Their Occurrence

There are fourteen such letters occurring in various combinations at the beginning of 29 *sūras*. The following is a list of their occurrence and distribution in the Qur'ān:

Alif Lām Rā': 10, 11, 12, 14, 15.
Alif Lām Mīm: 2, 3, 29, 30, 31, 32.
Alif Lām Mīm Rā': 13.
Alif Lām Mīm Ṣād: 7.

11 Qaṭṭān, M.: *mabāḥith fī 'ulūm al-qur'ān*, Riyādh, 1971.

12 *Itqān*, II, p.8 f. A summary of the orientalists' efforts on this topic is in Jeffery, Arthur: *The Mystic Letters of the Qur'ān*, *MW*, 14 (1924), pp. 247-60. Some of the orientalists suggested that the letters are abbreviations of the names of the various Companions who used to write the Qur'ān for Muḥammad. Still others say that the letters are simply symbols employed to distinguish the *sūra* from others before the now common names were introduced. *Sūra Ṭā Hā* would be a case in point. This is also based on some Muslim scholars' views (*Itqān*, II, p.10). Watt, the Edinburgh priest-orientalist, writes 'We end where we began; the letters are mysterious, and have so far baffled interpretation' (Watt, M.: *Bell's Introduction to the Qur'ān*, Edinburgh, 1977, p.64).

Hā Mīm: 40, 41, 43, 44, 45, 46.
Ṣād: 38.
Ṭā Sīn: 27.
Ṭā Sīn Mīm: 26, 28.
Ṭā Hā: 20.
Qāf: 50.
Kāf Hā Yā 'Ain Ṣād: 19.
Nūn: 68.
Yā Sīn: 36.

Variety of Explanations

The meaning and purpose of these letters is uncertain. There have been a variety of explanations offered by Muslim scholars throughout the ages. Among them are:[13]

— These letters might be abbreviations for certain sentences and words, such as e.g. *Alif Lām Mīm* meaning *Anā llāhu A'lam*; or *Nūn* meaning *Nūr* (light), etc.
— These letters are not abbreviations but symbols and names of Allah, or something else.[14]
— These letters have some numerical significance, as the semitic letters also have numerical value.
— These letters were used to attract the attention of the Prophet (and later his audience) for the revelation to follow.

There are also many other explanations which cannot be referred to here. The 'abbreviated letters' are part of the Qur'ānic message, revealed to the Prophet Muḥammad and therefore included in the text of the Qur'ān. They are to be recited and read as part of the *sūras* where they occur. They are a good example for one kind of *mutashābihāt* which is referred to in the Qur'ān itself, (3: 7), the meaning of which is known to Allah. The Qur'ān says of them: '. . . these are the symbols of the perspicuous book' (12: 1).

---

13 See *itqān*, II, pp.9-11.
14 e.g. the letter *nūn* standing for 'fish', which occurs in every *sūra* that has *nūn* as 'abbreviated letter' in front, or *ṭā* standing for snake, as every *sūra* with *ṭā* as 'abbreviated letter' in front contains the story of Mūsā and the snake.

CHAPTER 5

Understanding the Text

MAKKAN AND MADINAN REVELATIONS

The growth and development of the Muslim *umma* is marked by two great phases:

— The period in Makka, before the *hijra* (A.D. 622).

— The period in Madina, after the *hijra*.

Naturally the revelation from Allah to guide the Muslims also responded, to some extent, to these particular situations.

The Makkan Phase

The Makkan phase of the revelation lasted about 13 years, from the first revelation up to the *hijra*.

This phase is determined by the prime task of the Prophet to call people to Islam. The main themes of this call, based on the Qur'ānic revelation are:

— Allah and His unity (*tawḥīd*).

— The coming resurrection and judgement.

— Righteous conduct.

The role of the Prophet in this phase is in particular that of an announcer and warner.

The Madinan Phase

The Madinan phase lasted about ten years, from the *hijra* to the death of the Prophet. While the basic themes of the

Makkan phase remain, the factor of the Muslims' growing together into a community and the formation of the *umma*, now makes its presence clearly felt.

In Madina, there are four groups of people to be met:

— The *muhājirūn*, who migrated from Makka to Madina.

— The *anṣār*, who originated from Madina and helped the *muhājirūn*.

— The *munāfiqūn*, who are from Madina and pretended to support the Muslims.

— The *ahl al-kitāb*, i.e. Jews and Christians, with their respective scriptures.

In addition to these the Qur'ān also continued to address *al-nās*, 'mankind' i.e. all people, and referred to the disbelievers and ignorant ones.

Makkan and Madinan Sūras

Sūras of the Qur'ān have also been classified, according to their origin, into Makkan and Madinan *sūras*.

A *sūra* is said to be of Makkan origin, when its beginning was revealed in the Makkan phase, even if it contains verses from Madina.

A *sūra* is said to be of Madinan origin, when its beginning was revealed in the Madinan phase, even if it has verses from the Makkan period in its text.[1]

The following 85 *sūras* are, according to Zarkashī,[2] of Makkan origin:

96, 68, 73, 74, 111, 81, 87, 92, 89, 93, 94, 103, 100, 108, 102, 107, 109, 105, 113, 114, 112, 53, 80, 97, 91, 85, 95, 106, 101, 75, 104, 77, 50, 90, 86, 54, 38, 7, 72, 36, 25, 35, 19, 20, 56, 26, 27, 28, 17, 10, 11, 12, 15, 6, 37, 31, 34, 39, 40, 41, 42, 43, 44, 45, 46, 51, 88, 18, 16, 71, 14, 21, 23, 32, 52, 67, 69, 70, 78, 79, 82, 84, 30.

---

1 Mabānī, in GdQ, I, p.59.

2 Zarkashī, B.: *Al-burhān fī 'ulūm al-qur'an*, Cairo, 1958, Vol. 1, p.193.

There is a difference of opinion as to what was last revealed in Makka. Some say, following Ibn 'Abbās, that it was *Sūra* 29 (*al-'ankabūt*); others say *Sūra* 23 (*al-mu'minūn*); still others say *Sūra* 83 (*al-muṭaffifīn*). Some believe that *Sūra* 83 is actually Madinan.

The following 29 *sūras* are, according to Zarkashī,[3] of Madinan origin:

2, 8, 3, 33, 60, 4, 99, 57, 47, 13, 55, 76, 65, 98, 59, 110, 24, 22, 63, 58, 49, 66, 61, 62, 64, 48, 9, 5.

Some hold that *Sūra* 1 (*al-fātiḥa*) is of Makkan, others that it is of Madinan, origin.

The Makkan *sūras* constitute about 11, and the Madinan about 19 *juz'* of the text.

From the above division it is obvious that the Madinan *sūras* are the longer ones and comprise a much larger part of the Qur'ān.

Chronology

According to a list based upon Nu'mān b. Bashīr and given in the *fihrist* of al-Nadīm,[4] the chronological order of the revelation of the *sūras* is as follows:

96, 68, 73, 74, 111, 81, 94, 103, 89, 93, 92, 100, 108, 102, 107, 109, 105, 112, 113, 114, 53, 80, 97, 91, 85, 95, 106, 101, 75, 104, 77, 50, 90, 55, 72, 36, 7, 25, 35, 19, 20, 56, 26, 27, 28, 17, 11, 12, 10, 15, 37, 31, 23, 34, 21, 37, 40, 41, 47, 43, 44, 45, 46, 51, 88, 18, 6, 16, 71, 14, 32, 52, 67, 69, 70, 78, 79, 82, 84, 30, 29, 83, 54, 86.

Why is it important to know the chronology of the *sūras* and verses, although the Qur'ān is not arranged in chronological order?

To know the origin and order of some of the revelation is important for understanding its meaning which can often be more easily grasped if one knows the time and circumstances

---

3 Zarkashī, Vol. 1, p.194. For another list see *fihrist*, I, pp.52-3.

4 *Fihrist*, I, pp.49-52.

that relate to it. For instance, many *āyāt* from the Makkan period may be especially meaningful to Muslims living in a strongly un-Islamic environment, while some of the Madinan period would appeal much to Muslims who are in the process of formation of the *umma*. In some cases, unless one knows which of two or more related verses was revealed first, one cannot decide which legal ruling is now binding upon the Muslims. Here knowledge of the chronology is directly linked with the issue of *al-nāsikh wa al-mansūkh*.[5] It is also important to know the chronology of verses in order to understand the gradual development of many Muslim practices, attitudes and laws such as e.g. towards prohibition of alcohol, towards fighting, etc. and to see how these matters developed historically, i.e. during the lifetime of the Prophet in order to understand their full implications.[6]

Knowledge about the Makkan and Madinan *sūras* is derived from the *ṣaḥāba* and *tābi'ūn* and nothing is said about this by the Prophet himself.[7] This is because at his time everyone was a witness and well aware of the occasions of revelation.

Often there is internal evidence, as to which part of the revelation is Makkan or Madinan. There are a number of guiding criteria, which help to distinguish between them:

— The theme. Does it belong to the Makkan or Madinan period? e.g. verses about warfare (9: 5) are only revealed after *hijra*.

— Sometimes there is a direct reference, such as e.g. to Abū Lahab in *Sūra* 111, or to the Battle of Badr in *Sūra* 3: 123.

— The length. Makkan *āyāt* are often short, Madinan ones longer, e.g.: *Sūra al-shu'arā'* (26) is Makkan. It has 227 *āyāt*. *Sūra al-anfāl* (8) is Madinan. It has (only) 75 *āyāt*.

Makkan *sūras* are usually short, Madinan ones longer, e.g.:

---

5 See below for details.

6 For example as far as fighting the enemy is concerned, the first verse revealed on this particular subject is from *Sūra al-ḥajj* (22). This verse is from the Madinan period and it becomes clear from this that Muslims were not drawn to fight against the non-Muslims before the *hijra*. This has important implications for our own planning and thinking, e.g. to decide when Islam has to be defended today with verbal and when with physical means.

7 al-Bāqillānī, in Qaṭṭān, *op. cit.*, p.55.

Juz' 30 is overwhelmingly Makkan. It has 543 (Makkan) *āyāt*.

Juz' 18 is overwhelmingly Madinan. It has (only) 117 (Madinan) *āyāt*.

There are however exceptions in both cases.

— The form of address. Often the address: 'O ye who believe', and 'O people of the book' indicates a Madinan origin, while the addresses 'O Mankind' and 'O People' are usually of Makkan origin.

— The theme. Among the Makkan themes are *tawḥīd, shirk*, day of resurrection, moral corruption, stories of the Prophets. These topics are also found in Madinan *sūras*, but usually only touched upon briefly. Madinan themes which are not found in Makkan revelations are of social and legal implications, concerning marriage, divorce, inheritance, punishment, etc.

— There are 19 *sūras* with so-called *ḥurūf taḥajjī* (such as *alif*, *lām*, *mīm*, etc.). All these *sūras* are Makkan, except *Sūra al-baqara* (2) and *Āl 'Imrān* (3).

— All *āyāt* with the word *kallā* are Makkan.

— All *sūras* containing *sajda* are Makkan.

— Most of the *sūras* of the group *mufaṣṣal*, beginning with *Sūra qāf* (50) in the latter part of the Qur'ān are Makkan.

— All references to the *munāfiqūn* are from Madina (except *Sūra al-'ankabūt* (29). Its verse 11 is Makkan.

Summary

The knowledge of Makkan and Madinan revelations is one of the important branches of *'ulūm al-qur'ān*. It is not merely of historical interest, but particularly important for the understanding and interpretation of the respective verses.

Many *sūras* of the Qur'ān do contain material from both periods of revelation, and in some cases there exists difference of opinion among scholars concerning the classification of a particular passage. However, on the whole, it is a well-established distinction, fully employed in the science of *tafsīr* and best derived from the internal evidence of the text of the Qur'ān itself.

ASBĀB AL-NUZŪL

The Qur'ān has been revealed for guidance, for all times and situations to come. However, various *āyāt* were revealed at a particular time in history and in particular circumstances. The Arabic word *sabab* (pl. *asbāb*) means reason, cause and '*ma'rifa asbāb al-nuzūl*' is the knowledge about the reasons of the revelations, i.e. the knowledge about the particular events and circumstances in history that are related to the revelation of particular passages from the Qur'ān.

Its Importance

Wāḥidī (d. 468/1075), one of the best classical scholars in this field wrote: 'The knowledge about *tafsīr* of the *āyāt* is not possible without occupying oneself with their stories and explanation of (the reasons) for their revelation.'[8]

Knowledge about the *asbāb al-nuzūl* helps one to understand the circumstances in which a particular revelation occurred, which sheds light on its implications and gives guidance to the explanation (*tafsīr*) and application of the *āya* in question for other situations.

In particular, knowledge about the *asbāb al-nuzūl* helps one to understand:

- The direct and immediate meaning and implication of an *āya*, as it can be seen within its original context.
- The imminent reason underlying a legal ruling.
- The original intent of the *āya*.
- Whether the meaning of an *āya* is specific or of general application, and if so, under which circumstances it is to be applied.
- The historical situation at the time of the Prophet and the development of the early Muslim community.

Example:

'To God belong the East and the West: whithersoever ye

8 *Asbāb al-nuzūl*, by al-Wāḥidī al-Nīsābūrī, Cairo, 1968, p.4.

turn, there is the presence of God, for God is all-pervading, all-knowing' (2: 115).

Without knowing the *sabab* (reason), one might easily conclude that this revelation permits the Muslim to face any direction when performing prayer, while it is well known that to face *qibla* is one of the conditions without which prayer becomes invalid. The circumstances in which this revelation occurred explains its implications:

According to Wāḥidī[9] a group of Muslims travelled on a dark night and they did not know where the *qibla* was, so they later realised that they had prayed in the wrong direction. They asked the Prophet about it and he kept silent until the above verse was revealed.[10] Taking into account this reason for the revelation one cannot come to the wrong conclusion that it is unimportant where to turn in prayer. The scholars say however that this verse excuses the mistake of those who unwillingly and under adverse circumstances fail to observe the correct *qibla*.

How it is Known

The well-known *asbāb al-nuzūl* have been related to us by the reliable Companions of the Prophet Muḥammad. Only

9 *op.cit.*, pp.20-1.

10 Based on a report from Jābir b. 'Abdullāh. Wāḥidī also informs us about some other situations when the *āya* reportedly applied:

— That one may pray voluntary prayer on one's riding camel, in whichever direction it may turn (based on Ibn 'Umar).

— That the Companions of the Prophet asked why they were ordered to pray for the dead Negus of Abyssinia, who had prayed towards a different *qibla* than their own (based on Ibn 'Abbās and 'Atā').

— That the Jews asked, why the *qibla* of the Muslims had been changed from *bait al-maqdis* (based on Ibn Abī Ṭalḥa).

See Wāḥidī, *op.cit.*, p.21. All this supports the view (to which in particular K. Murad drew my attention) of Suyūṭī based on Zarkashī (Suyūṭī, *Lubāb an-nuqūl*, Tunis, 1981, p.7.) that when the *ṣaḥāba* of the Prophet spoke about an *āya* of the Qur'ān, saying 'It was revealed concerning. . .'(*nazalat fī kādhā*) they do not restrict themselves to narrating a single 'cause' for the revelation of an *āya* but rather refer to the 'situations' to which particular verses where found applicable during the lifetime of the Prophet while the occasion of the first revelation of the *āya* may have been much earlier. In this lie great avenues for understanding and *tafsīr* of the Qur'ānic message.

reports which are *ṣaḥīḥ* can be considered fully reliable, as is the case in the science of *ḥadīth* generally. A particular condition here is also that the person who relates it should have been present at the time and occasion of the event (the revelation).[11] Reports from *tābi'ūn* only, not going back to the Prophet and his Companions are to be considered weak (*ḍa'īf*). Hence one cannot accept the mere opinion of writers or people that such and such verse might have been revealed on such and such occasion. Rather one needs to know exactly who related this incident, whether he himself was present, and who transmitted it to us.

Kinds of Reports

There are two kinds of reports on *asbāb al-nuzūl*:

— Definite reports.

— Probable reports.

In the first kind (definite) the narrator clearly indicates that the event he relates is the *sabab al-nuzūl*.

Example:

> Narrated Ibn 'Abbās: the verse 'Obey Allah and obey the apostle and those of you (Muslims) who are in authority. . .' (4: 59) was revealed in connection with 'Abdullāh bin Ḥuḍāfa bin Qais bin 'Adī when the Prophet appointed him as the commander of a sariyya (army detachment).[12]

In the second kind (probable) the narrator does not indicate clearly that the event narrated is the *sabab al-nuzūl*, but suggests this probability.

Example:

> Narrated 'Urwa: Az-Zubair quarrelled with a man from the Anṣār because of a natural mountainous stream at Al-Ḥarra. The Prophet said: O Zubair, irrigate (your

---

11 Wāḥidī, p.4.

12 Bukhārī, VI, No. 108.

land) and then let the water flow to your neighbour. The Anṣār said: O Allah's apostle (this is because) he is your cousin? At that the Prophet's face became red (with anger) and he said: O Zubair. Irrigate (your land) and then withhold the water till it fills the land up to the walls and then let if flow to your neighbour. So the Prophet enabled Az-Zubair to take his full right after the Anṣārī provoked his anger.

The Prophet had previously given an order that was in favour of both of them. Az-Zubair said: 'I don't think but this verse was revealed in this connection: But no, by your Lord, they can have no faith, until they make you judge in all disputes between them' (4: 65).[13]

Kinds of Reasons

There are three kinds of 'reasons' which are connected with revelation of particular passages from the Qur'ān:

1 Revelation in response to an event or a general situation.
2 Revelation in response to a particular question that has been asked by someone.
3 Revelation for other reasons, known or not known to us.

Examples:

Response to an Event

Narrated Ibn 'Abbās: The Prophet went out towards Al-Baṭḥā' and ascended the mountain and shouted: 'O Sabāḥāh', so the Quraish people gathered around him. He said: 'Do you see? If I tell you that an enemy is going to attack you in the morning or in the evening, will you believe me?' They replied: 'Yes'. He said: 'Then I am a plain warner to you of a coming severe punishment'. Abū Lahab said: 'Is it for this reason that you have gathered us? May you perish!' Then Allāh revealed 'Perish the hands of Abū Lahab' (*Sūra* 111: verse 1).[14]

13 Bukhārī, VI, No. 109.
14 Bukhārī, VI, No. 496.

The *sūra* concerning Abū Lahab was revealed in response to this event, when Abū Lahab said: 'May you perish!'

Response to a Particular Situation

Sūra 2: 158 concerning Ṣafā and Marwā was revealed in response to a particular situation in Makka during the time of the Prophet.

> Narrated 'Urwa: I asked 'Ā'isha (regarding the Sa'ī between Aṣ-Ṣafā and Al-Marwā). She said: 'Out of reverence to the idol Manāt which was placed in Al-Mushallal those who used to assume Iḥrām in its name, used not to perform Sa'ī between Aṣ-Ṣafā and Al-Marwā (because there were two other idols between these two hills). So Allāh revealed: Verily Aṣ-Ṣafā and Al-Marwā are among the symbols of Allāh.' Thereupon Allāh's apostle and the Muslims used to perform Sa'ī (between them). Sufyān said: The (idol) Manāt was at Al-Mushallal in Qudaid. 'Ā'isha added: 'The verse was revealed in connection with the Anṣār. They and (the tribe of) Ghassān used to assume Iḥrām in the name of Manāt before they embraced Islam'. 'Ā'isha added 'There were men from the Anṣār who used to assume Iḥrām in the name of Manāt which was an idol between Makka and Medina. They said, O Allah's Apostle! We used not to perform the Ṭawāf (sa'ī) between Aṣ-Ṣafā and Al-Marwā out of reverence to Manāt.'[15]

In response to this situation 2: 158 was revealed.

Question to the Prophet

On many occasions the Muslims addressed questions to the Prophet concerning Islamic beliefs and the Islamic way of life. An example of the many occasions when a revelation was revealed in response to such a question posed to the Prophet is *Sūra* 4: 11:

---

15 Bukhārī, VI, No. 384; also Nos. 22, 23.

> Narrated Jābir: The Prophet and Abū Bakr came on foot to pay me a visit (during my illness) at Banū Salama's (dwellings). The Prophet found me unconscious, so he asked for water and performed the ablution from it and sprinkled some water over me. I came to my senses and said O Allah's apostle! What do you order me to do as regards my wealth?
>
> So there was revealed 'Allah commands you as regards your children's (inheritance)' (4: 11).[16]

The verse in question is concerned with inheritance and explains the rules of inheritance for children as follows:

> God (thus) directs you as regards your children's (inheritance):
>
> 'To the male a portion equal to that of two females: if only daughters, two or more, their share is two-thirds of the inheritance. If only one, her share is half. . .' (4: 11).

Question by the Prophet

On other occasions, the Prophet himself asked questions. *Sūra* 19: 64 was revealed in response to such a question by the Prophet Muḥammad:

> Narrated Ibn 'Abbās: The Prophet said to the Angel Gabriel, What prevents you from visiting us more often than you visit us now? So there was revealed: 'And we (angels) descend not but by the command of your Lord. To Him belongs what is before us and what is behind us . . .' (19: 64).[17]

Response to a General Question

There are numerous occasions when revelation was sent down providing guidance concerning general questions that had arisen in the Muslim community.

---

16 Bukhārī, VI, No. 101.
17 Bukhārī, VI, No. 255.

Thābit narrated from Anas: Among the Jews, when a woman menstruated, they did not dine with her, nor did they live with them in their houses; so the Companions of the apostle (may peace be upon him) asked the apostle (may peace be upon him) and Allah the Exalted revealed:

'And they ask you about menstruation: say it is a pollution, so keep away from women during menstruation' to the end (Qur'ān 2: 222).

The messenger of Allah (may peace be upon him) said: Do everything except intercourse. . .[18]

This report is also a good example of how the Prophet himself explained the meanings of the revelation when such questions arose.

Particular Persons

Often a general rule which became part of the Qur'ānic revelation, was first revealed in response to the circumstances or needs of a particular person, e.g. *Sūra* 2: 196:

'. . . And if any of you is ill, or has an ailment in his scalp (necessitating shaving) he should in compensation either fast or feed the poor or offer sacrifice. . .' Ka'b bin 'Ujra said this verse – and if one of you is ill or has an ailment in his scalp, – was revealed concerning me. I had lice on my head and I mentioned this to the Prophet and he said: Shave (your head) and compensate by fasting three days or a sacrifice or feed six poor, for each poor one *Ṣā'*.[19]

This is again an example of the Prophet himself explaining the revelation in detail. At other times such revelation could not be applied but to the respective person. The best example of such a revelation is *Sūra Lahab* (111) already referred to above. Other examples are references to the Prophet Muḥammad in the Qur'ān, such as e.g. *Sūra* 75: 16:

18 Muslim, I, No. 592.
19 Muslim, II, Nos. 2735, 2738, 2739; Wāḥidī, *op.cit.*, p.31. One *ṣā'* is a cubic measure of approx. 2.6kg.

Narrated Ibn 'Abbās (as regards Allāh's statement) 'Move not your tongue concerning (the Qur'ān) to make haste therewith' (75: 16).

When the Angel Gabriel revealed the divine inspiration to Allāh's Apostle he moved his tongue and lips, and that stage used to be very hard for him, and that movement indicated that revelation was taking place. So Allāh revealed in *Sūra al-qiyāma* which begins: 'I do swear by the Day of Resurrection . . .'

The Verses: 'Move not your tongue concerning (the Qur'ān) to make haste therewith. It is for us to collect it (Qur'ān) in your mind and give you the ability to recite it by heart' (75: 16-17).[20]

Several Asbāb and One Revelation

From the reports of the *ṣaḥāba* it appears that particular passages of the Qur'ān were revealed in response to more than one event, situation or question, or that the application of a particular passage of the Qur'ān was for more than one particular occasion, as pointed out above.

Examples:

Sūra al-ikhlāṣ (112) firstly responds to the *mushrikūn* in Makka before the *hijra*, and secondly to the *ahl al-kitāb* encountered in Madina after the *hijra*.[21]

Another example is *Sūra* 9: 113:

This *āya* was revealed firstly in connection with the death of the Prophet's uncle Abū Ṭālib, where Muḥammad said 'I will keep on asking (Allah for) forgiveness for you unless I am forbidden to do so'. Then there was revealed: it is not fitting for the Prophet and those who believe that they should pray for forgiveness for pagans, even though they be of kin, after it has become clear to them that they are the companions of the Fire.[22]

---

20 Bukhārī, VI, No. 451.
21 *Itqān*, I, p.35; Wāḥidī, *op.cit.*, pp.262-3.
22 Bukhārī, VI, No. 197.

The other occasion reported is when the Companions and in particular 'Umar b. al-Khaṭṭāb found the Prophet shedding tears when he visited the graveyard. The Prophet explained that he had visited his mother's grave and that he had asked his Lord's permission to visit it which had been granted to him and that he had also asked his Lord's permission to pray for her forgiveness which had not been granted to him and the above *āya* had been revealed.[23]

Several Revelations and One Sabab

A well-known example for several revelations, which are connected with one particular circumstance, are three verses which according to reliable reports, came down in response to the question of Umm Salama, whether or why only the men had been referred to in the Qur'ān, as being rewarded. According to Al-Ḥākim and Tirmidhī the verses 3: 195, 4: 32 and 33: 35 were revealed in response to this question:

> 'And their Lord has accepted of them and answered them: Never will I suffer to be lost the work of any of you be he male or female: Ye are members, one of another: those who have left their homes, or have been driven out therefrom, or suffered harm in My cause, or fought or been slain – verily I will blot out from them their iniquities and admit them into gardens with rivers flowing beneath; a reward from the presence of God and from His presence is the best of rewards' (3: 195).

> 'And in no wise covet those things in which God has bestowed His gifts more freely on some of you than on others; to men is allotted what they earn and to women what they earn: but ask God of His bounty for God has full knowledge of all things' (4: 32).

> 'For Muslim men and women – for believing men and women – for devout men and women, for true men and women, for men and women who are patient and constant, for men and women who humble themselves, for

23 Wāḥidī, *op.cit.*, p.152.

men and women who give in charity, for men and women who fast, for men and women who guard their chastity, and for men and women who engage much in God's praise – for them has God prepared forgiveness and great reward' (33: 35).[24]

Several Views on Sabab al-Nuzūl

It also occurs that the Companions of the Prophet when mentioning a revelation, differed in their views about its *sabab al-nuzūl*. This is due to the fact that as already shown above there have been various *asbāb* for one particular revelation, and each of the persons reporting the circumstances had been present only on one of the various occasions.

Otherwise several views about the same revelation have to be judged on their merits according to the rules of *'ulūm al-ḥadīth*, and one of them will be found to be stronger than the others.

Example:

There are two reports concerning the revelation of *Sūra* 17: 85:

According to Ibn 'Abbās, as reported in Tirmidhī, the Quraish asked the Jews to give them something they could ask the Prophet about and they were advised to ask about the Spirit (*al-rūḥ*). Then the *āya* 17: 85 was revealed.

From Ibn Mas'ūd, as reported in Bukhārī, it is related that he said:

> While I was in the company of the Prophet on a farm, and he was reclining on a palm leaf stalk, some Jews passed by. Some of them said to the others: Ask him about the Spirit. Some of them said: What urges you to ask him about it. Others said: (Don't) lest he should give you a reply which you dislike, but they said, Ask him. So they asked him about the Spirit. The Prophet kept quiet and did not give them any answer. I knew that he was being divinely inspired so I stayed at my place. When the

24 Ṣāliḥ, *op.cit.*, p.148.

divine inspiration had been revealed, the Prophet said 'They ask you (O Muḥammad) concerning the Spirit. Say: "the Spirit", its knowledge is with my Lord and from the knowledge it is only a little that has been given to you (mankind)' (17: 85).

The second report, although the first one has been declared *ṣaḥīḥ* by Tirmidhī, is considered to be stronger because it comes from Ibn Mas'ūd, who says that he was present on the occasion of the revelation, while the report from Ibn 'Abbās in Tirmidhī does not contain this information.[25]

Specific or General?

Another question leads directly to the field of *tafsīr*, but is still connected with *asbāb al-nuzūl*. When one knows about the *sabab al-nuzūl*, it is still to be decided whether the revelation has a specific implication for the particular occasion it was connected with, or whether it is of general implication and needs to be applied by all Muslims at all times.

Example:

> 'As to the thief, male or female, cut off his or her hands: a punishment by way of example, from God, for their crime: and God is exalted in power' (5: 41).

This verse although it was revealed concerning a specific person who had stolen a piece of armour and had been punished accordingly, is of general application.[26]

What is not Asbāb al-Nuzūl

In some cases scholars have provided us with the background of certain events that have been narrated in the Qur'ān. Obviously, however, such information does not belong to the field of *asbāb al-nuzūl*. Although it may help to understand the message of the revelation, it is not related in a

25 See Ṣāliḥ, op.cit., pp.145-6; Bukhārī, VI, No. 245.
26 See Wāḥidī, *op.cit.*, p.111; also Tafsīr Ibn al-Jauzī, Beirut, 1964, Vol.II, p.348.

direct and reliable way, showing immediate reason for or the occasion of the revelation.

Example:

> 'Seest thou not how thy Lord dealt with the companions of the elephant?' (105: 1).

The following passage from a book of *tafsīr*, although it contains information about the background of the event narrated in the *sūra*, does not belong to the field of *asbāb al-nuzūl*:

> (The companions of the elephant) had come from the Yemen and wanted to destroy the *Ka'ba* (they were) from Abyssinia and their leader was Abraha al-Ashram, the Abyssinian.[27]

Summary

The branch of *'ulūm al-qur'ān* concerned with the *asbāb al-nuzūl* is one of the most important areas of knowledge for the proper understanding and explanation of the Qur'ānic revelation. The message of the Qur'ān is guidance for all times. However its *āyāt* were revealed at particular points of time in history and in particular circumstances.

One of the most crucial steps in meaningful interpretation is to distinguish between that part which is attached solely to the historical event and that part, which, although attached to the historical event, also has wider implications. The knowledge of *asbāb al-nuzūl* helps to distinguish between these two by:

- Clarifying the events and circumstances, which are connected with the revelation of certain *āyāt*.
- Illustrating the application of such *āyāt* by referring to situations, when the Companions of the Prophet found them proper and applicable.

27 Tujībī, *mukhtaṣar min tafsīr al-Ṭabarī*, Cairo, 1970, II, p.529.

The revelations from Allah as found in the Qur'ān touch on a variety of subjects, among them beliefs, history, tales of the prophets, day of judgement, Paradise and Hell, and many others. Particularly important are the *aḥkām* (legal rulings), because they prescribe the manner of legal relationships between people, as Allah wishes them to be observed.

While the basic message of Islam remains always the same, the legal rulings have varied throughout the ages, and many prophets before Muḥammad brought particular codes of law (*sharī'a*) for their respective communities.

The Arabic words '*nāsikh*' and '*mansūkh*' are both derived from the same root word '*nasakha*' which carries meanings such as 'to abolish, to replace, to withdraw, to abrogate'.

The word *nāsikh* (an active participle) means 'the abrogating', while *mansūkh* (passive) means 'the abrogated'. In technical language these terms refer to certain parts of the Qur'ānic revelation, which have been 'abrogated' by others. Naturally the abrogated passage is the one called '*mansūkh*', while the abrogating one is called '*nāsikh*'.

The Qur'ān on Naskh

The principle of *naskh* (abrogation) is referred to in the Qur'ān itself and is not a later historical development:

> 'None of Our revelations do We abrogate or cause it to be forgotten, but We substitute something better or similar: knowest thou that God has power over all things?' (2: 106).[28]

How it came about

When the message of Islam was presented to the Arabs as something new, and different from their way of life, it was

28 Some however say that this refers to the revelations before the Qur'ān, which have now been substituted by the Qur'ān itself. See Mawdūdī, *The Meaning of the Qur'ān*, Lahore, 1967, Vol. 1, p.102, note 109.

introduced in stages. The Qur'ān brought important changes gradually, to allow the people to adjust to the new prescriptions.

Example:

There are three verses in the Qur'ān concerning the drinking of wine. Wine drinking was very widespread in pre-Islamic times and, although a social evil, highly esteemed. The three verses which finally led to the prohibition of intoxicating substances were revealed in stages (4: 43, 2: 219; 5: 93-4).

Why it is important

Knowledge of *al-nāsikh wa al-mansūkh* is important because it concerns the correct and exact application of the laws of Allah. It is specifically concerned with legal revelations:

— It is one of the important pre-conditions for explanation (*tafsīr*) of the Qur'ān.

— It is one of the important pre-conditions for understanding and application of the Islamic law (*ḥukm, sharī'a*).

— It sheds light on the historical development of the Islamic legal code.

— It helps to understand the immediate meaning of the *āyāt* concerned.

Tafsīr (explanation of the Qur'ān) or legal ruling is not acceptable from a person who does not have such knowledge.

How do we know it?

As in the field of *asbāb al-nuzūl*, the information about *al-nāsikh wa al-mansūkh* cannot be accepted upon mere personal opinion, guesswork or hearsay, but must be based on reliable reports, according to the *'ulūm al-ḥadīth*, and should go back to the Prophet and his Companions.

The report must also clearly state which part of the revelation is *nāsikh* and which is *mansūkh*.

Some scholars say that there are three ways of knowing about *al-nāsikh wa al-mansūkh*:

1 Report from the Prophet or Companions.
2 *Ijmā'* (consensus of the *umma* upon what is *nāsikh* and what *mansūkh*).
3 Knowledge about which part of the Qur'ān preceded another part in the history of revelation.[29]

Example:

Narrated Mujāhid (regarding the verse):

> Those of you who die and leave wives behind, they (their wives) shall await (as regards their marriage) for four months and ten days (2:234).
>
> The widow, according to this verse, was to spend this period of waiting with her husband's family, so Allah revealed: Those of you who die and leave wives (i.e. widows) should bequeath for their wives, a year's maintenance and residence without turning them out, but if they leave (their residence) there is no blame on you for what they do with themselves, provided it is honourable (i.e. lawful marriage) (2:240).
>
> So Allah entitled the widow to be bequeathed extra maintenance for seven months and 20 nights and that is the completion of one year. If she wished, she could stay (in her husband's home) according to the will, and she could leave it if she wished, as Allah says: Without turning them out, but if they leave (the residence) there is no blame on you.
>
> So the idea (i.e. four months and ten days) is obligatory for her.
>
> 'Aṭā' said: Ibn 'Abbās said: This verse i.e. the statement of Allah . . . without turning one out . . . cancelled the obligation of staying for the waiting period in her late husband's house, and she can complete this period wherever she likes.

29 Qaṭṭān, *op.cit.*, p.199.

'Aṭā' said: If she wished, she could complete her 'idda by staying in her late husband's residence according to the will or leave it according to Allah's statement:

'There is no blame on you for what they do with themselves.'

'Aṭā' added: Later the regulations of inheritance came and abrogated the order of the dwelling of the widow (in her dead husband's house) so she could complete the 'idda wherever she likes. And it was no longer necessary to provide her with a residence.

Ibn 'Abbās said: This verse abrogated her (i.e. the widow's) dwelling in her dead husband's house and she could complete the 'idda (i.e. four months and ten days) (wherever she liked, as Allah's statement says: . . . 'without turning them out. . .'[30]

This report explains clearly which part of the revelation is *nāsikh* and which is *mansūkh*. Mujāhid was one of the well-known *tābi'ūn* and Ibn 'Abbās was a Companion of the Prophet.

What is Abrogated?

According to some scholars the Qur'ān abrogates only the Qur'ān. They base their view on *sūras* 2: 106 and 16: 101. According to them the Qur'ān does not abrogate the *sunna* nor does the *sunna* abrogate the Qur'ān. This is, in particular, the view held by Shāfi'ī.[31]

Others are of the opinion that the Qur'ān may abrogate the Qur'ān as well as the *sunna*. They base their view on *Sūra* 53: 3-4.

There is also the view that there are four classes of *naskh*:

1 Qur'ān abrogates Qur'ān.

---

30 Bukhārī, VI, No. 54.

31 For details see *Kitāb al-risāla*, Cairo, n.d., pp.30-73; English translation by M. Khadduri, *op.cit.*, pp.123-45; for a brief summary of Ash-Shāfi'ī's views see also Seeman, K., *Ash-Shāfi'īs Risala*, Lahore, 1961, pp.53-85.

2 Qur'ān abrogates *sunna*.
3 *Sunna* abrogates Qur'ān.
4 *Sunna* abrogates *sunna*.[32]

In this discussion, we shall only consider the abrogation in the Qur'ān, and leave aside the abrogation in the *sunna*.

Three Kinds of Naskh in the Qur'ān[33]

The scholars have divided abrogation into three kinds:

1 Abrogation of the recited (verse) together with the legal ruling.
2 Abrogation of the legal ruling without the recited (verse).
3 Abrogation of the recited (verse) without the legal ruling.

Examples:

For abrogation of the recited (verse) together with its legal ruling:

> 'Ā'isha (Allah be pleased with her) reported that it had been revealed in the Holy Qur'ān that ten clear sucklings make the marriage unlawful, then it was abrogated (and substituted) by five sucklings and Allah's apostle (may peace be upon him) died and it was before that time (found) in the Holy Qur'ān (and recited by the Muslims).[34]

For abrogation of a legal ruling without the recited (verse):

> 'O Prophet! We have made lawful to thee thy wives to whom thou has paid their dowers; and those whom thy right hand possesses out of the prisoners of war whom God has assigned to thee; and daughters of thy paternal uncles and aunts and daughters of thy maternal uncles and aunts, who migrated (from Makka) with thee; and any believing woman who dedicates her soul to the

32 Qaṭṭān, *op.cit.*, pp.201-2.
33 Ibn Salāma, *al-nāsikh wa al-mansūkh*, Cairo, 1966, p.5.
34 Muslim, II, No. 3421.

Prophet if the Prophet wishes to wed her; – this only for thee and not for the believers (at large); We know what we have appointed for them as to their wives and the captives whom their right hands possess; – in order that there should be no difficulty for thee and God is oft-forgiving, most merciful' (33: 50).

'It is not lawful for thee (to marry more) women after this, nor to change them for (other) wives, even though their beauty attract thee, except any thy right hand should possess (as handmaidens); and God doth watch over all things' (33: 52).

This is one of the few very clear examples of *naskh*, though only concerning the Prophet specifically, since for Muslims in general the number of wives has been restricted to four. (*Sūra* 4: 3).

For abrogation of the recited (verse) without the legal ruling:

'Abdullāh bin 'Abbās reported that 'Umar bin Khaṭṭāb sat on the pulpit of Allah's messenger (may peace be upon him) and said: Verily Allah sent Muhammad (may peace be upon him) with truth and he sent down the book upon him, and the verse of stoning was included in what was sent down to him. We recited it, retained it in our memory and understood it. Allah's messenger (may peace be upon him) awarded the punishment of stoning to death (to the married adulterer and adulteress) and after him, we also awarded the punishment of stoning. I am afraid that with the lapse of time, the people (may forget it) and may say: We do not find the punishment of stoning in the book of Allah, and thus go astray by abandoning this duty prescribed by Allah. Stoning is a duty laid down in Allah's book for married men and women who commit adultery when proof is established, or if there is pregnancy or a confession.[35]

The punishment of stoning for adultery by married people

35 Muslim, III, No. 4194; Bukhārī, VIII, No. 816.

has been retained in the *sunna*, while it is not included in the Qur'ān.

The Abrogated Verses

There are, according to Ibn Salāma,[36] a well-known author on the subject:

— 43 *sūras* with neither *nāsikh* or *mansūkh*.
— 6 *sūras* with *nāsikh* but no *mansūkh*.
— 40 *sūras* with *mansūkh* but no *nāsikh*.
— 25 *sūras* with both *nāsikh* and *mansūkh*.

According to Suyūṭī's *itqān* there are 21 instances in the Qur'ān, where a revelation has been abrogated by another. He also indicates that there is a difference of opinion about some of these: e.g. 4:8, 24:58, etc.[37]

Some scholars have attempted to reduce the number of abrogations in the Qur'ān even further, by explaining the relationships between the verses in some special ways, e.g. by pointing out that no legal abrogation is involved, or that for certain reasons the *naskh* is not genuine.

Shāh Walīullāh (d. 1759) the great Muslim scholar from India only retained the following 5 out of Suyūṭī's 21 cases as genuine:

Mansūkh 2:180	*nāsikh* 4:11, 12.
Mansūkh 2:240	*nāsikh* 2:234.
Mansūkh 8:65	*nāsikh* 8:62.
Mansūkh 30:50	*nāsikh* 33:52.
Mansūkh 58:12	*nāsikh* 58:13.

Example:

A case listed by Suyūṭī, which has no direct legal implication is the following:

> Narrated Ibn 'Abbās: When the verse: 'If there are 20 amongst you, patient and persevering, they will over-

---

36 *Op.cit.*, see pp.6-8 for the names of these *suras*.
37 *Itqān*, II, pp.20-3; Kamāl, *op.cit.*, pp.101-9 also gives Suyūṭī's complete list.

come two hundred', was revealed, it became hard on the Muslims, when it became compulsory that one Muslim ought not to flee before 10 (non-Muslims) so Allah lightened the order by revealing: 'but now Allah has lightened your (task) for He knows that there is weakness in you. But (even so) if there are 100 amongst you who are patient and persevering, they will overcome 200 (non-Muslims)' (8: 66).

So when Allah reduced the number of enemies that Muslims should withstand, their patience and perseverence against the enemy decreased as much as their task was lightened for them.[38]

Still others hold that there are no genuine (*ṣaḥīh*) reports available on this issue, going back to the Prophet, while those going back to the Companions contradict each other.[39] Therefore to them the issue of *nāsikh wa al-mansūkh* is perhaps not of great importance. However, it is clear from the Qur'ān itself, (e.g. in the case of inheritance, 2: 180; 4: 7-9, etc.) that abrogation occurred occasionally. Hence it is wrong to completely ignore the subject.

Abrogation and Specification

There is of course a difference between abrogation and specification. By the latter is meant that one revelation

38 Bukhārī, VI, No.176.

39 Ali, M.M.: *The Religion of Islam*, Lahore, 1936, p.32. It may be pointed out that Ali's treatment of the subject is not very thorough. Of the three examples he cites in support of his opinion ('in most cases, where a report is traceable to one Companion who held a certain verse to have been abrogated, there is another report traceable to another Companion, through the fact that the verse was not abrogated' – p.33) two are definitely not in his favour, while the third can be easily explained. His first case concerns *Sūra* 2: 180 (inheritance). It has certainly been superseded by other verses, e.g. 4: 7-9 and that is probably all that is meant, when saying it is *mansūkh*. Ali's second case, '2: 184, is considered by Ibn 'Umar as having been abrogated while Ibn 'Abbās says it was not'. See below, where I have quoted this very *ḥadīth* from Ibn 'Abbās (Bukhārī, VI, No.32) where Ibn 'Abbās himself explains *why* he does not hold it as abrogated. The third case is, like the first one, definitely not in support of Ali: '2: 240 was abrogated according to Ibn Zubair, while Mujāhid says it was not'. This is wrong, see *Ṣaḥīḥ* Bukhārī, VI, Nos. 53 and 54, where both Ibn Zubair and Mujāhid hold the verse to be abrogated. Furthermore both Ibn Zubair and Mujāhid are *tābi'ūn*, and not Companions (*ṣaḥāba*).

explains in more detail or according to specific circumstances how another revelation should be understood.

Example:

Sūra 2: 183 says 'O you who believe, fasting is prescribed to you. . .'

> Narrated 'Aṭā' that he heard Ibn 'Abbās reciting the Divine verse 'for those who can do it is a ransom, the feeding of one that is indigent' (2: 184).
>
> Ibn 'Abbās said 'This verse is not abrogated but it is meant for old men and old women who have no strength to fast, so they should feed one poor person for each day of fasting (instead of fasting).[40]

It is quite clear that the second verse (2: 184) does not abrogate the rule of fasting from the first verse (2: 183) but explains that in a specific case, that of feeble old people, there is a way of making up for the loss of fast.

In the same way the verses concerning intoxicating drinks can be understood as specifications rather than abrogations (see 4: 43; 2: 219; 5: 93-4).

Summary

The Qur'ān, in 2: 106, refers to the concept of *naskh*. However, there is a difference of opinion about the extent to which *al-nāsikh wa-al mansūkh* does in fact occur in the text of the Qur'ān. The information concerning *al-nāsikh wa-al mansūkh* must be treated with great caution as, for all reports concerning the text of the Qur'ān, two independent witnesses are required. Many of the examples which the scholars have drawn upon to illustrate this question (and I have quoted them for the same purpose) are based on *one* witness only. 'Ā'isha *alone* reported that 10 or 5 sucklings had been part of the Qur'ānic recitation, and *only* 'Umar reported that the 'verse of stoning' had been included in the Qur'ānic text. These legal rulings are *not* included in the Qur'ān precisely because they were not considered reliable, being based on

40 Bukhārī, VI, No. 32.

one witness only. Similarly, other examples about *naskh*, based on the words of Ibn 'Abbās or Mujāhid *alone*, are to be judged by the same measure.

However, as mentioned there remain a small number of verses which, as far as can be ascertained from the internal evidence of the Qur'ān, have been superseded by other verses in the Qur'ān.

VARIETY OF MODES

What is the meaning of *al-aḥruf al-sab'a*?

The word *sab'a* means seven, and *aḥruf* is the plural form of *ḥarf,* which has many meanings, among them 'edge' border, letter, word', etc. In technical language it describes the *variety of modes* of the Qur'ān transmitted to us, also expressed in various forms of writing the text.

Example:

Read the two versions of *Sūra* 2:9 given on plates 7 and 8. Disregard the difference in style of writing. The first example is from a Qur'ān from North Africa, the second from a Qur'ān from Jordan. In the North African version, the word '*yukhadi'ūna*' (they deceive) is used twice, while in the Jordan version, the word occurs as '*yakhda'ūna*' in the second instant. Both are correct and accepted readings, since they have been transmitted to us. Also there is no objection from the viewpoint of grammar or correct language and the writing without vowel signs can carry both readings.

The Language of the Quraish

In the time of the Prophet Muḥammad when the Qur'ān was revealed, the Arab tribes scattered all over the peninsula, spoke a number of dialects, each containing peculiar words and idioms.

The language of the Quraish had developed into a form of 'high Arabic' due to the many influences it absorbed, being spoken at the main centre of trade and pilgrimage in Arabia.

Hence this language was obviously the most suitable to carry the messages of revelation which were to reach all peoples and not be restricted to a particular tribe.

The Seven Modes

The *ḥadīth* reports tell us that the Qur'ān was actually revealed in seven modes (*al-aḥruf al-sab'a*). This has been narrated by more than ten of the Prophet's Companions, among them Abū Bakr, 'Umar, 'Uthmān, Ibn Mas'ūd, Ibn 'Abbās and others.[41]

The following is the *ḥadīth* in Bukhārī:

> 'Narrated 'Abdullāh bin 'Abbās: Allah's apostle said: Gabriel recited the Qur'ān to me in one way. Then I requested him (to read it in another way), and continued asking him to recite it in other ways, and he recited it in several ways till he ultimately recited it in seven different ways'.[42]

On another occasion, 'Umar complained to the Prophet that Hishām had recited *Sūra al-furqān* in a way different from what 'Umar had heard from the Prophet, but the Prophet said: '. . . this Qur'ān has been revealed to be recited in seven different ways, so recite of it whichever is easier for you'.[43]

Salmān is reported to have said that he read a passage from 5:82 in the presence of the Prophet in the following two versions, the first of which is now in the Qur'ānic text, while the second constitutes a variant reading according to 'Ubay b. Ka'b:[44]

1 *dhālika bi-anna minhum qissīsīna wa ruhbānā.*

2 *dhālika bi-anna minhum* ṣiddiqīna *wa ruhbānā.*[45]

Muslim scholars have put forward a number of explanations and benefits for the Muslim *umma* deriving from the revelation

41 *Itqān*, I, p. 41.
42 Bukhārī, VI, No. 513.
43 Bukhārī, VI, No. 514.
44 Ibn Abī Dāwūd, p.129.
45 *ibid.*, p.103.

of the Qur'ānic message in several modes. Among these the following are most important:

— To make the reading, pronunciation and memorisation more easy, as many people were illiterate in the Prophet's time.
— To unite the new Muslim community on the basis of one common language, the Arabic of the Quraish, with minor variations accepted, according to spoken language.
— To show something of the unique nature of the Qur'ān, in the realm of language.
— To show something of the unique nature of the Qur'ān, in the realm of meaning and legal rulings.
— To explain a legal ruling in more detail.

Scholars Differ

There is a difference of opinion among classical Muslim scholars on the subject of the 'seven modes', to the extent that one of them was able to say: 'the degree of difference of opinion (*ikhtilāf*) among the scholars is to the extent of 35 sayings'.[46]

Some of these different opinions are that the 'seven modes' are:

— Different languages (dialects) current among the Arabs at the time of revelation, such as e.g. Quraish, Hudhail, Tamīm, etc., who had different ways of pronunciation, which could even affect the spelling, e.g.
al-tabuh and *al-tabūt*. (2:248)[47]
or: *hiyāka* for *iyāka* (1:5).
or: *attā* for *hattā* (12:35).
— It may also be the usage of words from the different languages in the Qur'ān (this is considered one of the most sound views).
— Usage of synonyms in the Qur'ān, i.e. that a variety of

---

46 *Itqān*, I, p.45.
47 See Kamāl, *op.cit.*, p.46.

expressions describe one and the same concept. A well-known example is *Sūra* 101: 5, which reads as '*Ka-l-'ihni-l-manfūsh*', but in another version '*Ka-ṣ-ṣūfi-l-manfūsh*' both meaning 'like carded wool'. The word *arshidnā* was read in place of *ihdinā* (*Sūra* 1: 6), etc.[48]

— Different aspects of the revelation, such as e.g. order, prohibitions, promise, narrations, etc.

— Seven differences, such as possible ways of reading words and structures in the Qur'ān, e.g. the word 'trusts' in 23: 8 which can be read both 'trust' (sg.) or 'trusts' (pl.) according to the plain text without vowels: *li-amānatihim* or *li-amānātihim*.

— Slightly different wordings of a particular passage, such as e.g. in 9: 100: 'Gardens under which rivers flow' which some read as 'Gardens from under which rivers flow', adding the word 'from' (*min*) to the text.

— Different ways of pronunciation as they have been explained in great detail by the scholars of *qirā'a* (recitation) such as e.g. *imāla*, *idghām*, etc.[49]

However, even non-Muslim orientalists concede that 'no major differences of doctrines can be constructed on the basis of the parallel readings based on the 'Uthmanic consonantal outline, yet ascribed to *muṣḥafs* other than his. All the rival readings unquestionably represent one and the same text. They are substantially agreed in what they transmit. . .'.[50]

Summary

From these different opinions, of which only some have been listed above, by way of illustration, a generally-accepted conclusion is that the 'seven modes' are at the basis of several distinct ways of *reciting the Qur'ān*, reflecting the different usage at the time of revelation, comprising variations in pro-

48 Both examples from Ibn Mas'ūd. This view is also very close to the idea of various dialects, and many scholars tend to accept such usage of synonyms, as meaning the 'seven modes'.

49 This view has also been favoured by many, because it does not cause much controversy.

50 Burton, J.: *The Collection of the Qur'ān*, Cambridge, 1977, p.171.

nunciation and even minor differences in wording. The 'seven *'aḥruf*' are however, not identical with the well-known 'seven readings'. These came about in a later age. Although much of what the 'seven readings' contain is also found in the seven *aḥrūf*, there are some differences, which will be explained when discussing the seven readings.

Only a few examples for *'aḥruf*' have been transmitted to us. They are of importance for *tafsīr*, rather than *qirā'a*.

Seven Modes in the Qur'ān

While some scholars[51] hold that the written Qur'ān now includes only one of the 'seven modes', and the others are transmitted orally to us, there is some evidence also for the view that the text of the Qur'ān, as we have it in front of us, may include all these 'seven modes' because:

— No one would change the Qur'ān.
— The present text was written upon the basis of the *ṣaḥāba* testimonies, both orally and written, going back directly to the Prophet.
— The Qur'ān is protected by Allah.

THE VARIOUS READINGS

Al-qirā'a (pl. *qirā'āt*) is derived from the word *qara'a*, 'reading, reciting'; from which also the word Qur'ān is derived. It is a verbal noun, meaning recitation. In technical language it describes the oral recitation of the Qur'ān as well as the punctuation of the written text, which corresponds to the oral recitation.

Examples:

---

51 e.g. Ṭabarī, *Jāmi' al-bayān 'an ta'wīl āyāt al-qur'ān*, Cairo, 1968. See introduction to this *tafsīr*. Zarkashī, Vol. 1, p.213 says most scholars are of the first view, and that the last double-reading of the Qur'ān by Muḥammad in the presence of the Angel Gabriel served, among others, the purpose of eliminating the other six modes.

Mawdūdī[52] has very convincingly explained the proper understanding of some accepted difference in reading. He wrote that in *al-fātiḥa* (1:3):

— *maliki*
— *māliki*

both describe one of the attributes of Allah, and there is absolutely no contradiction between 'sovereign' and 'master' of the day of judgement, but 'these two readings make the meaning of the verse all the more clear'.

Similarly 5:8 *arjulakum*[53] and *arjulikum*[54] carry two meanings:

— Wash
— Wipe

your feet

Both are indeed correct, for under normal circumstances a man will wash his feet, while some other person e.g. a traveller may wipe them. Here the text of the Qur'ān carries both meanings at the same time. This is indeed a unique feature of the revelation from Allah.

Readers among the Ṣaḥāba

Reading and reciting of the Qur'ān has been done since revelation began, and the Prophet was the first to recite. This has already been discussed in the section on transmission of the text. After his death, the recitation continued through his Companions. Among the famous readers from whom many of the *tābi'ūn* learned, were 'Ubay bin Ka'b, 'Alī, Zaid bin Thābit, Ibn Mas'ūd, Abū Mūsā al-Ash'arī and many others.

Later Development

Later on, with Muslims settling in many parts of the world, the Qur'ān was recited in a variety of ways, some of which were not in accordance with the accepted text and the transmitted readings from the Prophet and the Companions. This

52 *Introduction to the Study of the Qur'ān*, Delhi, 1971, p.21.
53 Reading of Nāfi', Ḥafṣ *'an* 'Āṣim, Kisā'ī.
54 Reading of Ibn Kathīr, Abū 'Amr, Abū Bakra *'an* 'Āṣim, Ḥamza.

necessitated a thorough screening and distinction between what is *ṣaḥīḥ* (sound) and what is *shādh* (exceptional).

The Seven Readings

The 'seven readings' were standardised in the second/eighth century. Ibn Mujāhid, a ninth-century Muslim scholar, wrote a book entitled *The Seven Readings*, in which he selected seven of the prevailing modes of recitation as the best transmitted and most reliable. Others were subsequently disfavoured and even opposed, among them the readings of Ibn Mas'ūd and 'Ubay bin Ka'b. However, this is not to say that one must restrict oneself to one of these seven readings, or to all of them. Below are listed the local origin of the seven readings and the names of readers[55] and some transmitters (*rāwis*) connected with them:

	Place	Reader	Transmitter
1	Madina	Nāfi' (169/785)	Warsh (197/812)
2	Makka	Ibn Kathīr (120/737)	
3	Damascus	Ibn 'Āmir (118/736)	
4	Basra	Abū 'Amr (148/770)	
5	Kufa	'Āṣim (127/744)	Ḥafṣ (180/796)
6	Kufa	Ḥamza (156/772)	
7	Kufa	Al-Kisā'ī (189/804)	Dūrī (246/860)

Readings No. 1 and 5 are of particular importance: the reading transmitted by Warsh is widespread in Africa, except Egypt, where, as now in almost all other parts of the Muslim world, the reading transmitted by Ḥafṣ is observed.

Other Views

Later on other views emerged, making ten or fourteen well-known readings. In addition to the seven above, the following make up the ten and the fourteen readers:

---

55 For their short biographies see *Fihrist,* I, p.63ff.

8	Madina	Abū Ja'far (130/747)
9	Basra	Ya'qūb (205/820)
10	Kufa	Khalaf (229/843)
11	Basra	Ḥasan al-Baṣrī (110/728)
12	Makka	Ibn Muḥaiṣin (123/740)
13	Basra	Yaḥyā al-Yazīdī (202/817)
14	Kufa	al-A'mash (148/765)

The readings are also divided as follows:[56]

— The *mutawātir* (transmitted by many; they include the seven well-known readings).

— The *āḥād* (transmitted by one; they number three, going back to the *ṣaḥāba* and together with the seven make up the ten).

— The *shādh* (exceptional; they go back to the *tābi'ūn* only).

Muslim scholars have laid down three criteria for the acceptance of any *qirā'a* and three criteria for preferring some over others. The best transmission was of course *mutawātir*. The three criteria for acceptance of other readings are:

— Correctness according to Arabic grammar.

— Agreement with the written text of 'Uthmān.

— Traced back reliably to the Prophet.

The three criteria for preference are:

— Correctness according to Arabic grammar.

— Agreement with the written text of 'Uthmān.

— Reported/preferred by many (majority).

Summary

The best summary on this topic is perhaps contained in the words of the scholar Abu-l-Khair bin al-Jazarī (d.833/1429), who wrote:

56 Suyūṭī, *itqān*, I, p.77.

'Every reading in accordance with Arabic (grammar) even if (only) in some way, and in accordance with one of the *maṣāḥif* of 'Uthmān, even if (only) probable, and with sound chain of transmission, is a correct (*ṣaḥīḥ*) reading, which must not be rejected, and may not be denied, but it belongs to the seven modes (*aḥruf*) according to which the Qur'ān was revealed, and the people are obliged to accept it, no matter whether it is from the seven *Imāms*, or the ten or from other accepted *Imāms*, but when one of these three conditions is not fulfilled, it must be rejected as weak (*ḍa'īf*) or exceptional (*shādh*) or void (*bāṭil*), no matter whether it is from the seven or from one who is older than them.'[57]

---

57 Suyūṭī, *itqān*, I, p.75.

CHAPTER 6

Interpreting the Text

TAFSĪR, ITS KINDS AND PRINCIPLES

Tafsīr (exegesis) of the Qur'ān is the most important science for Muslims. All matters concerning the Islamic way of life are connected to it in one sense or another since the right application of Islam is based on proper understanding of the guidance from Allah. Without *tafsīr* there would be no right understanding of various passages of the Qur'ān.

Tafsīr and Ta'wīl

The word *tafsīr* is derived from the root *'fassara'* – to explain, to expound. It means 'explanation' or 'interpretation'. In technical language the word *tafsīr* is used for explanation, interpretation and commentary on the Qur'ān, comprising all ways of obtaining knowledge, which contributes to the proper understanding of it, explains its meanings and clarifies its legal implications.[1] The word *mufassir* (pl. *mufassirūn*) is the term used for the person doing the *tafsīr*, i.e. the 'exegete' or 'commentator'.

The word *ta'wīl*, which is also used in this connection, is derived from the root *'awwala'* and also means 'explanation, interpretation'.

In technical language it similarly refers to explanation and interpretation of the Qur'ān.

Tafsīr in the language of the scholars means explanation and clarification. It aims at knowledge and understanding concerning the book of Allah, to explain its meanings, extract

1 See Zarkashī, *op.cit.*, I, p.13.

its legal rulings and grasp its underlying reasons. *Tafsīr* explains the 'outer' (*ẓāhir*) meanings of the Qur'ān. *Ta'wīl* is considered by some to mean the explanation of the inner and concealed meanings of the Qur'ān, as far as a knowledgeable person can have access to them. Others are of the opinion that there is no difference between *tafsīr* and *ta'wīl*.

Why is it Important?

There are a number of reasons why *tafsīr* is of great importance, but the basic reason is the following: Allah has sent the Qur'ān as a book of guidance to mankind. Man's purpose is to worship Allah, i.e. to seek His pleasure by living the way of life Allah has invited him to adopt. He can do so within the framework of the guidance that Allah has revealed concerning this, but he can do so only if he properly understands its meanings and implications.

A Warning

Some Muslim scholars have warned against *tafsīr*. Aḥmad b. Ḥanbal, e.g. has said: 'Three matters have no basis: *tafsīr*, *malāḥim* (tales of eschatological nature) and *maghāzī* (tales of the battles)'.[2]

By this is meant that there is much exaggeration and unsound material in these fields, but it does not mean that neither of them ought to be considered. This is clear from another version of the same verdict, in which the word *isnād* is used for 'basis'.

Basic Conditions

Muslim scholars have laid down certain basic conditions for sound *tafsīr*. Any *tafsīr*, which disregards these principles must be viewed with great caution, if not rejected altogether. The most important among these conditions are the following:

The *mufassir* must:

2 Ibn Taimīya, *muqaddima fī uṣūl al-tafsīr*, Kuwait, 1971, p.59.

— Be sound in belief (*'aqīda*).
— Well-grounded in the knowledge of Arabic and its rules as a language.
— Well-grounded in other sciences that are connected with the study of the Qur'ān (e.g. *'ilm al-riwāya*).
— Have the ability for precise comprehension.
— Abstain from the use of mere opinion.
— Begin the *tafsīr* of the Qur'ān with the Qur'ān.
— Seek guidance from the words and explanations of the Prophet.
— Refer to the reports from the *ṣahāba*.
— Consider the reports from the *tābi'ūn*.
— Consult the opinions of other eminent scholars.

Grades of Sources[3]

The best *tafsīr* is the explanation of the Qur'ān by the Qur'ān.

The next best is the explanation of the Qur'ān by the Prophet Muḥammad, who, as Shāfi'ī explained, acted according to what he understood from the Qur'ān.

If nothing can be found in the Qur'ān nor in the *sunna* of the Prophet, one turns to the reports from the *ṣaḥāba*.[4]

If nothing can be found in the Qur'ān, the *sunna* and the reports from the *ṣaḥāba*, one turns to the reports from the *tābi'ūn*.[5]

However, nothing can match the explanation of the Qur'ān by the Qur'ān and the explanation of the Qur'ān by the Prophet.

Kinds of Tafsīr

— *Tafsīr* may be divided into three basic groups:[6]

3 See Ibn Taimīya, *op.cit.*, p.93.
4 *ibid.*, p.95.
5 *ibid.*, p.102.
6 This classification has been borrowed from Ṣābūnī, *tibyān*, p.63. See also Qaṭṭān, *op.cit.*, section 25.

— *Tafsīr bi-l-riwāya* (by transmission), also known as *tafsīr bi-l-ma'thūr*.
— *Tafsīr bi'l-ra'y* (by sound opinion; also known as *tafsīr bi-l-dirāya*, by knowledge).
— *Tafsīr bi-l-ishāra* (by indication, from signs).

Tafsīr bi-l-riwāya

By this is meant all explanations of the Qur'ān which can be traced back through a chain of transmission to a sound source, i.e.:
— The Qur'ān itself.
— The explanation of the Prophet.
— The explanation by Companions of the Prophet (to some extent).

Naturally, the explanation of the Qur'ān by the Qur'ān and the explanation of the Qur'ān by the Prophet are the two highest sources for *tafsīr*, which cannot be matched nor superseded by any other source. Next to these rank the explanations by the *ṣaḥāba*, since the *ṣaḥāba* were witnesses to the revelations, were educated and trained by the Prophet himself and were closest to the period of the first Muslim *umma*. Of course all reports of explanations by the Prophet or by a *ṣaḥābī* must be sound according to the science of *riwāya* as in *'ulūm al-ḥadīth*.

The Qur'ān explained by the Qur'ān. The interpretation of the Qur'ān by the Qur'ān is the highest source of *tafsīr*. Many of the questions which may arise out of a certain passage of the Qur'ān have their explanation in other parts of the very same book, and often there is no need to turn to any sources other than the word of Allah, which in itself contains *tafsīr*. To seek to explain an *āya* from the Qur'ān by referring to another *āya* from the Qur'ān is the first and foremost duty of the *mufassir*. Only if this does not suffice, he will refer to other sources of *tafsīr*.[7]

---

7 *Itqān*, II, pp.181-2.

Examples:

A case in point is the detailed explanation of 5:2 by 5:4, concerning permissible and prohibited meat. Another example of explanation of one *āya* in the Qur'ān by another concerns a question which might arise from *Sūra* 44:3. It is explained in *Sūra* 97:1:

> 'We sent it down during a blessed night' (44:3).

Which night is this blessed night, in which the Qur'ān was sent down?

> 'We have indeed revealed this in the *lailat al-qadr*' (97:1).

A third example is the explanation of *Sūra* 2:37 by *Sūra* 7:23:

> 'Then learnt Adam from his Lord words of inspiration, and his Lord turned towards him, for He is Oft-Returning, Most Merciful' (2:37).

These 'words of inspiration' are explained by the Qur'ān as follows:

> 'Our Lord! We have wronged our own souls. If Thou forgive us not, and bestow not upon us Thy mercy, we shall certainly be lost' (7:23).

The Qur'ān explained by the Prophet. There are numerous examples of explanation of the Qur'ān by the Prophet, who either himself asked the Angel Gabriel for explanation of matters not clear to him, or who was asked by the Companions about the Qur'ān. Suyūṭī has given a long list of explanations of the Qur'ān by the Prophet *sūra* by *sūra*.[8]

Here one example may suffice:

> 'And eat and drink until the white thread of dawn appears to you distinct from its black thread...' (2:187).

> Narrated 'Adi b. Ḥātim: I said: 'O Allah's Apostle! What

---

8 *Itqān*, II, pp.191-205.

is the meaning of the white thread distinct from the black thread? Are these two threads?' He said: 'You are not intelligent, if you watch the two threads'. He then added, 'No, it is the darkness of the night and the whiteness of the day'.[9]

Tafsīr by Ṣaḥāba.[10] Next, after explanation of the Qur'ān by the Qur'ān and of the Qur'ān by the Prophet himself, ranks the explanation of the Qur'ān by the *ṣaḥāba*. Among them, the following were best known for their knowledge of and contribution to the field of *tafsīr*: Abū Bakr, 'Umar, 'Uthmān, 'Alī (not much has been reported from them), Ibn Mas'ūd, Ibn 'Abbās, 'Ubay b. Ka'b, Zaid b. Thābit, Abū Mūsā al-Ash'arī, 'Abdullāh b. Zubair.

Ibn 'Abbās. Abdullāh b. 'Abbās (d. 68/687) is considered to be the most knowledgeable of the Companions in *tafsīr*.[11] He has been called *'tarjumān al-qur'ān'*, the interpreter of the Qur'ān. Since he was related to the Prophet, being his cousin, and his maternal aunt Maimūna being one of the Prophet's wives, he was very close to the Prophet Muḥammad and learnt much about the revelation. It is said that he saw the Angel Gabriel twice. Apart from his detailed knowledge of everything concerning *tafsīr*, he is also given the credit for having emphasised one of the basic principles of *'ilm al-tafsīr* which has remained important to this day, namely, that the meaning of words, especially of unusual words in the Qur'ān ought to be traced back to their usage in the language of pre-Islamic poetry. There is a long list of such explanations quoted by Suyūṭī.[12]

Example:

The following is an example of *tafsīr* from a *ṣaḥābī*, namely Ibn 'Abbās, confirmed by 'Umar:

---

9 *Itqān*, II, pp.191-205.

10 For a brief summary on early *tafsīr*, see al-Ṣawwāf, 'Early Tafsīr', in Ahmad, K. and Z. I. Ansari: *Islamic Perspectives*, Leicester, 1979, pp.135-45.

11 A book entitled *tanwīr al-miqbās min tafsīr Ibn 'Abbās* (Beirut, n.d.) is a complete *tafsīr* of the Qur'ān, all explanations of which are said to go back to Ibn 'Abbās. On the question of authenticity, see al-Ṣawwāf, *op.cit.*, p.140.

12 *Itqān*, I, pp.120-33.

'So celebrate the praises of your Lord, and ask for His forgiveness. Verily! He is the one who accepts the repentance and forgives' (110: 3).

Narrated Ibn 'Abbās: 'Umar used to make me sit with the elderly men who had fought in the battle of Badr. Some of them felt it (did not like that) and said to 'Umar: 'Why do you bring in this boy to sit with us, while we have sons like him?'

'Umar replied 'Because of what you know of his position' (i.e. his religious knowledge).

One day 'Umar called me and made me sit in the gathering of those people, and I think that he called me just to show them (my religious knowledge). 'Umar then asked them in my presence: 'What do you say about the interpretation of the statement of Allāh'.

'When comes help of Allāh, and the conquest . . .' (110: 1).

Some of them said: 'We are ordered to praise Allāh and ask for His forgiveness, when Allah's help and the conquest (of Makka) comes to us'. Some others kept quiet and did not say anything. On that 'Umar asked me: 'Do you say the same, O Ibn 'Abbās?' I replied: 'No'. He said: 'What do you say then?' I replied: 'That is the sign of the death of Allāh's apostle which Allāh informed him of. Allāh said:

'(O Muḥammad) when comes the help of Allāh (to you against your enemies) and the conquest (of Makka) (which is the sign of your death) – you should celebrate the praises of your Lord and ask for His forgiveness, and He is the One who accepts the repentance and forgives' (110: 1-3). On that 'Umar said: 'I do not know anything about it other than what you have said'.[13]

Another short example is:

Narrated 'Aṭā': When Ibn 'Abbās heard:

---

13 Bukhārī, VI, No. 494.

'Have you not seen those who have changed the favour of Allāh into disbelief?' (14: 28).

He said: 'Those were the disbelieving pagans of Makka.'[14]

Tafsīr by Tābi'ūn. There are many more persons from among the *tābi'ūn* known for their preoccupation with *tafsīr*, because many more people had embraced Islam and the need for knowledge about the Qur'ān had increased manifold. Also, the Prophet himself and many of his Companions were no longer available to give this guidance, and therefore greater efforts had to be made to satisfy this need for proper understanding of the book of Allah.

Of the *mufassirūn* from among the *tābi'ūn* one distinguishes three groups, according to their origin and area of activity:

— Those from Makka.
— Those from Madina.
— Those from Iraq.

The Makkan Group. According to many scholars, this group of *mufassirūn* from among the *tābi'ūn* are the most knowledgeable in *tafsīr*, because they learnt about it from 'Abdullāh b. 'Abbās. They are many in number, and among the best known out of many others are Mujāhid (d.104/722), 'Atā' (d.114/732) and 'Ikrima (d.107H).

Mujāhid, the best known among them, is reported to have gone through the Qur'ān thrice with Ibn 'Abbās and to have asked him about the 'when' and 'how' of each verse that had been revealed.[15]

A complete book of *tafsīr* by Mujāhid has been published. It is based on a manuscript from the 6th Hijra century and is edited by Surtī.[16]

Example:

Humaid b. Qais Makki reported: I was with Mujāhid and

---

14 Bukhārī, VI, No. 222.
15 Taimīya, p.102.
16 Surtī, A.: *Tafsīr Mujāhid*, 2 vols., Beirut, n.d.

we were circumambulating the house (Ka'ba). A man came and asked whether the fasts of penalty of an oath should be observed continuously or severally. Humaid replied that if he liked he could observe them severally too! But Mujāhid said: Not severally, for the reading of 'Ubayy b. Ka'b is thalāthi ayyāmin mutatābi'āt, i.e. to fast three days continuously'.[17]

The Madinan Group. The *mufassirūn* among the *tābi'ūn* from Madina had many Companions as their teachers, among the best known being 'Ubay b. Ka'b. The following are some of the well-known Qur'ān exegetes among them: Muḥammad b. Ka'b al-Qarzī (d.117/735), Abū-l 'Allīya al-Riyaḥī (d.90/708) and Zaid b. Aslam (d.130/747).

The Iraq Group. There were also many *mufassirūn* among the *tābi'ūn* in Iraq. Their principal teacher was Ibn Mas'ūd. Their main centres were Basra and Kufa. The best known among them are: Al-Ḥasan al-Baṣrī (d.121/738), Masrūq b. al-'Ajda' (d.63/682) and Ibrāḥīm al-Nakha'ī (d.95/713).

Summary

Nothing can excel the *tafsīr* of the Qur'ān by the Qur'ān. This is followed by sound reports about the Prophet's explanation of the revelation.

Whatever is sound and genuine in the explanation of the Qur'ān by the *ṣaḥāba* and the *tābi'ūn* may not be rejected, but the following principles are to be observed:

— Sound reports must be distinguished from unsound ones, for many views have been falsely attributed to some *ṣaḥāba* and *tābi'ūn* (especially to Ibn 'Abbās and Mujāhid, the most renowned ones among them), which cannot be traced back to them when the *isnād* is investigated. Those reports must of course be rejected.

— Material from the *ahl-al-kitāb*, in particular the Jewish traditions (*isrā'īliyāt*)[18] must be sorted out and evaluated.

---

17 *Muwaṭṭa'* Mālik, No. 617.
18 For details, see below, p. 133.

— Material which crept in due to theological, philosophical, political and other considerations, must be sorted out and evaluated (such as e.g. some *Shī'a* attributions to 'Alī, or 'Abbasid attributions to Ibn 'Abbās, etc.).

— False material purposely introduced by the enemies of Islam must be distinguished from sound material.

Tafsīr bi'l-ra'y

The second kind of *tafsīr*, after *tafsīr bi'l-riwāya*, is the so-called *tafsīr bi'l-ra'y*. It is not based directly on transmission of knowledge by the predecessors, but on the use of reason and *ijtihād*.

Tafsīr bi'l-ra'y does not mean 'interpretation by *mere* opinion', but deriving an opinion through *ijtihād based on sound sources*. While the former has been condemned already in the *ḥadīth*, the latter is recommendable, when used in its proper place as sound *ijtihād*, and was also approved by the Prophet, e.g. when he sent Mu'ādh bin Jabal to Yemen.[19]

Tafsīr bi'l-ra'y on the other hand has been declared *ḥarām* on the basis of the following *ḥadīth*:

> 'From Ibn 'Abbāṣ: Allah's messenger said: "He who says (something) concerning the Qur'ān without knowledge, he has taken his seat of fire"'.[20]

However this *ḥadīth* has been explained in two ways:

— That no one should say of the Qur'ān what is not from the *ṣaḥāba* or *tābi'ūn*.

— That no one should say of the Qur'ān what he knows to be otherwise.[21]

The obvious meaning of the *ḥadīth* is that one should not say something about the Qur'ān without having the proper knowledge, the sources of which have already been explained.[22]

---

19 *Mishkāt al-maṣābīḥ*, *op.cit.*, II, p.794: (Arabic), Vol. 2, No. 3737.

20 Ibn Taimīya, p.105, from Tirmidhī, who says it is *ḥasan ṣaḥīḥ*.

21 Ṣābūnī, *tibyān*, p.174.

22 The Qur'ān explained by the Qur'ān, by the Prophet, by the Companions, by the *tābi'ūn*, by sound *ijtihād*.

Two Kinds of tafsīr bi'l-ra'y. In view of this, it is obvious that *tafsīr bi'l-ra'y* should not be rejected in toto, but is acceptable if based on sound *ijtihād*.[23] Scholars have therefore grouped *tafsīr bi'l-ra'y* into two kinds:

— *Tafsīr maḥmūd* (praiseworthy), which is in agreement with the sources of *tafsīr*, the rules of *sharī'a* and the Arabic language.

— *Tafsīr madhmūm* (blameworthy), which is done without proper knowledge of the sources of *tafsīr*, *sharī'a* and the Arabic language. It is therefore based on mere opinion and must be rejected.

Ṣaḥāba and Tābi'ūn shun mere opinion. While the *tafsīr bi'l-ra'y* based on sound sources was accepted, it is reported that from the outset the *ṣaḥāba* had refused to involve themselves in giving explanations based on mere opinion:

> It is reported that a man asked Ibn 'Abbās about the day (mentioned in the Qur'ān) which measures 50 years, and Ibn 'Abbās replied: 'They are 2 days which Allah has mentioned in His book, and Allah knows best about them', and he disliked that he should say concerning the book of Allah, what he did not know.[24]

The same attitude is also found among the *tābi'ūn*:

> 'We used to ask Sa'īd b. al-Musayyib about ḥalāl and ḥarām, and he was the most learned man, but when we asked him about *tafsīr* of a verse of the Qur'ān, he kept silent, as though he did not hear.'[25]

Summary

Some scholars have said that *tafsīr bi'l-ra'y* is not allowed. since it cannot be traced back to the Prophet or his

---

23 Someone who practises *tafsīr bi'l-ra'y* must have sound knowledge in the following fields: *'ilm al-balāgha, 'ilm uṣūl al fiqh, ma'rifat asbāb al-nuzūl, ma'rifat al-nāsikh wa-l-mansūkh, 'ilm al-qirā'a*. Also, he must be inclined towards faith, which is a gift from Allah, and not a skill to be acquired.

24 Ibn Taimīya, p.110, based on Ṭabarī.

25 Ibn Taimīya, p.112, based on Ṭabarī.

Companions directly. Others, who form the majority, say that it is permissible under the conditions described briefly above, because it is done by *ijtihād*, based on sound sources, which is a permissible means of obtaining knowledge.

Tafsīr bi-l-ishāra

By this is meant the interpretation of the Qur'ān beyond its outer meanings, and the people practising it concern themselves with meanings attached to verses of the Qur'ān, which are not visible to anyone, but only to him whose heart Allah has opened. This kind of *tafsīr* is often found with mystically-inclined authors. While it must not be denied that Allah guides to the understanding of the Qur'ān whom He pleases and as He wills, it has to be said that *tafsīr bi-l-ishāra* is not a matter of science and scientific principles, which may be acquired and then used, as are the other branches of *'ulūm al-qur'ān* and of *tafsīr*. Some scholars have therefore rejected it from the viewpoint of general acceptability and said it is based on mere opinion.[26] However Ibn al-Qayyim[27] is reported to have said that results achieved by *tafsīr bi-l-ishāra* are permissible and constitute good findings, if the following four principles are jointly applied:

— That there is no disagreement with the plain meaning of the verse.

— That it is a sound meaning in itself.

— That in the wording there is some indication towards it.

— That there are close connections between it and the plain meaning.

Differences in Tafsīr

In some cases the *mufassirūn* do not agree on the interpretation of a given verse from the Qur'ān. There are a number of reasons for this, the most important ones are the following:

---

26 *Itqān*, II, p.174.
27 Qaṭṭān, *op.cit.*, pp.309-10.

— External: Disregard for *isnād*.

Use of unsound materials, such as *isrā'īliyāt*.[28]

Conscious misrepresentation, based on a preconceived belief or other ulterior motives.

— Internal: Genuine mistake in comprehension.

Interpretation based on unconscious preconceived notion.

Multiplicity of meanings in the revelation from Allah.

The main cause however is, in the view of Ibn Taimīya, that the people introduced false innovation (*bid'a*) and 'twisted the speech (of God) from its actual position, and interpreted the speech of Allah and His apostle(s) other than it is meant, and explained it other than it should be explained.'[29]

Isrā'īliyāt[30]

This word, meaning 'of Jewish origin' refers to explanations derived from non-Muslim sources and especially from the Jewish tradition, but also including other *ahl al-kitāb* in general. Such material was used very little by the *ṣaḥāba*, but more by the *tābi'ūn* and even more by later generations. There are many aspects of the Qur'ān which can be explained by referring to such sources, when there is common ground between the Qur'ān and the other traditions. However, the information taken from such sources must be used with great caution and cannot be considered sound according to the standards of *'ilm al-ḥadīth*, unless traced back to the Prophet himself and his Companions. The Prophet has already cautioned Muslims against this source of knowledge:

> Narrated Abū Huraira: The people of the scripture (Jews) used to recite the Torah in Hebrew and they used to explain it in Arabic to the Muslims. On that Allah's apostle said: 'Do not believe the people of the scripture

---

28 See below.
29 Ibn Taimīya, *op.cit.*, p.91.
30 See Ibn Taimīya, *op.cit.*, pp.56-8.

or disbelieve them, but say: "We believe in Allah and what is revealed to us"' (2: 136).

Similarly Ibn Mas'ūd, the well-known Companion, is reported to have said: 'Do not ask the *ahl al-kitāb* about anything (in *tafsīr*), for they cannot guide you and are themselves in error. . .'[31]

Hence one distinguishes three kinds of the so-called *isrā' īliyāt*:

— Those known to be true because the revelation to the Prophet Muḥammad confirms them.
— Those known to be false, because the revelation to the Prophet Muḥammad rejects them.
— Those not known to be true or false, and we do not say they are true or false.

Summary

A concise but useful summary of the vast field of *tafsīr* can be found in the following words said to be from Ibn 'Abbās:[32]

'*Tafsīr* has four aspects:

the aspect the Arabs knew because of its language,[33]
tafsīr, for ignorance of which no one will be excused,[34]
tafsīr, which the scholars know,
tafsīr, which no one knows except Allah'.

THE TAFSĪR LITERATURE

Some Important Books of Tafsīr

Numerous books have been written by Muslim scholars on

31 Ibn Taimīya, *op.cit.*, p.57.
32 Ibn Taimīya, p.115, based on Ṭabarī.
33 i.e. linguistic matters.
34 i.e. concerning *ḥarām* and *ḥalāl*.

the subject of *tafsīr*.[35] The oldest text available is attributed to Ibn 'Abbās (d.68/687) although some doubt its authenticity. Other old books of *tafsīr*, still available to us, include the works of Zaid bin 'Alī (d.122/740) and Mujāhid, the famous *tāb'ī* (d.104/722).[36]

However it is generally accepted that the *magnum opus* among the early books of *tafsīr*, which have come down to us is the *tafsīr* al-Ṭabarī.

Tafsīr al-Ṭabarī. This book was written by Ibn Jarīr al-Ṭabarī (d.310/922) under the title *jāmi' al-bayān fī tafsīr al qur'ān*. It belongs to the most famous books in *tafsīr* and is perhaps the most voluminous work we have on the subject. It belongs to the class of *tafsīr bi'l-riwāya* and is based on the reports from the Prophet, the *ṣaḥāba* and the *tābi'ūn*, giving the various chains of transmission and evaluating them. However, it also contains reports that are not sound, without clearly indicating this, including so-called *isrā'īliyāt*. Ṭabarī also says in some places that one cannot know about certain things and that not to know about them does not do any harm. In spite of all this the book is nevertheless one of the most important works in *tafsīr* referred to by almost every subsequent scholar. It has been printed twice in Egypt (in 1903 and 1911) in 30 volumes, while a third edition begun in 1954 has reached volume 15.

Other Well-Known Books of Tafsīr

— Tafsīr al Samarqandī, by Abū al-Laith al-Samarqandī (d.373/983) under the title *baḥr al 'ulūm* with many reports from the *ṣaḥāba* and *tabi'ūn*, but without *sanad*.

— Tafsīr al Tha'labī, by Aḥmad bin Ibrāḥīm al Tha'labī al Nīsābūrī (d.383/993) under the title *al kashf wa-l-bayān 'an tafsīr al-qur'ān* with some *sanad* and some unsound tales and stories.

— Tafsīr al-Baghawī, by Ḥasan bin Mas'ūd al-Baghawī

35 For extracts from the classical books of *tafsīr* translated into English see Gaetje, H.: *The Qur'ān and its Exegesis*, London, 1976.

36 See Ṣawwāf, *op.cit.*, pp.135-45.

(d.510/1116) under the title *ma'ālim al-tanzīl* being an abridgement of Tha'labī with its weaknesses but with more emphasis on soundness of *ḥadīth*.

— Tafsīr Ibn Kathīr, by Ismā'īl bin 'Amr bin Kathīr al Dimashqī (d.774/1372) under the title *tafsīr al-qur'ān al-aẓīm*, one of the better-known books on *tafsīr*, perhaps second to Ṭabarī, with more emphasis on soundness of reports, in particular rejection of all foreign influences such as *isrā'īliyāt*, discussing the *sanad* of various reports often in detail, which makes it one of the more valuable books of *tafsīr*. Makes much use of *tafsīr al-qur'ān bi'l qur'ān*, referring a reader to other relevant *āyāt* on the topic discussed. This book has been printed on various occasions (in 8 volumes) and an abridged version (*mukhtaṣar*) has been edited by Ṣābūnī. No English translation available. This book although of greatest importance to Muslims has been widely ignored by the orientalists.[37]

— Tafsīr al-Suyūṭī, by Jalāl al-Dīn al-Suyūṭī (d.911/1505) under the title *al-durr al-manthūr fī-l-tafsīr bi-l-ma'thūr*.

Some important books from the class of *tafsīr bi'l-ra'y* are as follows:

— *Al-kashshāf*, by Abu'l-Qāsim Maḥmūd Ibn 'Umar al Zamakhsharī (d.539/1144), one of the well-known books of *tafsīr* based on a *mu'tazila* approach and considered to be the standard work of *mu'tazila tafsīr,* with much emphasis on Arabic grammar and lexicography as a means of interpretation with less attention given to *sanad*.

— *Mafātiḥ al-ghaib,* by Muḥammad bin 'Amr al-Ḥusain al-Rāzī (d.606/1209). One of the most comprehensive works of *tafsīr bi'l-ra'y* covering many areas often beyond the actual field of exegesis, also known as the *tafsīr al-kabīr*.

---

37 See e.g. Gaetje, *op.cit.*, who does not even mention Ibn Kathīr's name. Also Goldziher, I.: *Die Richtungen der islamischen Koranslegung,* Leiden, 1970, is silent about him.

— *Anwār al-tanzil*, by 'Abd Allāh bin 'Umar al-Baiḍāwī (d.685/1286), a summary of Zamakhsharī with additional material to counterbalance the *mu'tazila* stance of the *kashshāf*.

— *Rūḥ al ma'ānī*, by Shihāb al-Dīn Muḥammad al-Ālūsī al-Baghdādī (d.1270/1854), criticises unsound reports; considered to be among the best of *tafsīr bi'l-ray'*.

— *Tafsīr al-Jalālain*, by Jalāl al-Dīn al-Maḥallī (d.864/1459) and Jalāl al-Dīn al-Suyūṭī (d.911/1505), a handy book of *tafsīr*, containing only brief notes on various passages of the Qur'ān.

None of these important books have ever been translated into any European language.[38]

To conclude, here is an example from the *tafsīr* al-Jalālain:[39]

> 'About the Hypocrites:
>
> Among men are those who say, we believe in God and in the Last Day – (that is the Day of Resurrection, because it is the last of days): but they are not believers. They endeavour to deceive God and those who have believed, by making a show of the reverse of the infidelity that they conceal; but they deceive not any except themselves; for the punishment of their deceit shall come upon them, and they shall be disgraced in this world, in consequence of God's acquainting His Prophet with that which they conceal, and shall be punished in the world to come; and they know not that they deceive themselves. In their hearts is a disease. Doubts and hypocrisy in this order

38 There are, however, a few extracts available in English, which may help the reader gain some idea of this important field of study: See Gaetje, *op.cit*.

39 Lane, Edward William: *Selection from the Kuran* . . . with an interwoven commentary, London, Madden, 1843. This is a most interesting though very rare book. Apart from a lengthy introduction (96 pages) almost wholly from Sale, it contains selections from the Qur'ān, translated into English with commentary taken from the *tafsīr* al-Jalālain. It therefore gives some idea of what this *tafsīr* is like. The selections reflecting the translator's cultural and historical millieu rather than the message of the Qur'ān are on the following topics: God and His Works, Predestination, Angels and Jinn, Various Prophets and Books, Messiah, Muḥammad and the Qur'ān, Believers and Unbelievers, Paradise and Hell.

them; and God has increased their disease by what he has revealed in the Kur-an, because they disbelieve it; and for them (is ordained) a painful punishment because they have charged with falsehood the Prophet of God and when it is said to them: corrupt not in the earth by infidelity and hindering others from embracing the faith – they reply, we are all only rectifiers – assuredly they are the corrupters; but they are not sensible thereof and when it is said unto them, believe ye as other men, the Companions of the Prophet, have believed – they say, shall we believe as the fools have believed? – assuredly they are the fools; but they know it not. And when they meet those who have believed they say, we believe; – but when they retire privately to their devils (that is, their chiefs), they say, we agree with you in religion; we only mock at them by making a show of their faith – God will mock at them. He will requite them for their mockery and continue them in their exceeding wickedness, wandering about in perplexity. These are they who have purchased error in exchange for right direction, and their traffic has not been profitable; on the contrary, they have incurred loss; for their transit is to the external fire; and they have not been rightly directed in that which they have done' (2: 7-15).[40]

Contemporary Tafsīr Literature[41]

Among numerous books on *tafsīr* that have been written in the twentieth century, three are outstanding. They have greatly influenced the thinking of Muslims all over the world, and are briefly introduced here. They are:

— *Tafsīr al-manār.*
— *Fī ẓilāl al-qur'ān.*
— *Tafhīm al-qur'ān.*

40 Lane, pp.285-7.

41 For a survey of the modern *tafsīr* literature as perceived by the orientalists, see Baljon, J. M. S.: *Modern Muslim Koran Interpretation*, Leiden, 1968, and Jansen, J. J. G.: *The Interpretation of the Qur'ān in Modern Egypt*, Leiden, 1974.

Tafsīr al-manār. The actual title of this book is *tafsīr al-qur'ān al-ḥakīm*. It was compiled by Muḥammad Rashīd Rīḍā (d.1354/1935), the well-known disciple of Muḥammad 'Abduh (d.1323/1905), and published in Egypt. It is called *tafsīr al-manār* since some of its parts had been serialised in the periodical *al-manār*. The *tafsīr* covers the first 12 *juz'* of the Qur'ān. The influence of the '*Manār* School of Thought' on Muslims all over the world since the turn of the century has been tremendous, although today, after several decades, some of the attempts to harmonise contemporary scientific as well as social development with the teachings of the Qur'ān seem rather inappropriate. For example, the commentary on *Sūra* 1:276, where Jinns are explained as microbes causing diseases, or on 4:3 where polygamy is 'prohibited' according to the *tafsīr al-manār*, because justice cannot be done between two or more wives. However the basic notion of the '*Manār* School of Thought' was that Islam is different and has to be seen as different from all Western philosophies and must regain its original position. This view, underlying the *tafsīr al-manār* continues to be voiced by many later Muslim scholars and leaders alike.[42]

Fī ẓilāl al-qur'ān. This book, covering the complete Qur'ānic text in 4 volumes, with the title *In the Shade of the Qur'ān* has greatly influenced numerous Muslims especially the younger generations, and particularly in the Middle East. It was written by the well-known author Sayyid Quṭb (d.1386/1966), mostly during his imprisonment (1954-64), and completed before he was executed by the Egyptian government because of his association with the *ikhwān al-muslimūn*.

Quṭb's aim, with this commentary on the Qur'ān was to explain the true nature of Islam to contemporary Muslims, so as to invite them to join the struggle for the establishment of Islam both on the individual as well as the social level. He emphasised in particular the differences that exist between Islam and the non-Islamic systems, as well as the need for Muslims to strive for the establishment of a movement for

---

42 Also *juz' 'amma* has been published. For a short extract on *Sūra* 4: 3, see Gaetje, *op. cit.*, pp.248-61.

Islam.[43]

Tafhīm al-qur'ān.[44] Written in Urdu, and first published in article form, from 1943, in the journal *tarjumān al-qur'ān*, this *tafsīr*, covering the complete Qur'ānic text was completed in 1973. It is of great importance for contemporary Muslim thinking, particularly in the Indian subcontinent (Pakistan, India, Bangladesḥ, Ceylon), but has also, by means of translation, reached a much wider audience.[45] This *tafsīr*, entitled *Understanding of the Qur'ān* was written by the well-known founder of the *Jamā'at-i-Islāmī* in Pakistan, Abul A'lā Mawdūdī (d.1400/1979). Addressed primarily to a non-Arabic speaking audience this *tafsīr* places great emphasis on the thorough explanation of basic Qur'ānic concepts, such as *ilāh, rabb, 'ibāda* and *dīn,* and the Qur'ān as a 'book of guidance', not least containing guidance for a movement of Islamic reconstruction and the Islamic way of life. Numerous notes add to the usefulness of this aid to understanding the Qur'ān. It is particularly suitable for the young educated Muslim with no direct access to the Arabic original.

Summary

There is a common factor in these three contemporary books. *Tafsīr al-manār* for the first time in modern history attempted to relate, to some extent, the Qur'ānic message to the actual situation of the Muslim *umma* in the contemporary world, and here, for the first time for centuries, *tafsīr* is no longer restricted to purely academic exercise and intellectual stimulus, but regains social and political significance. This is upheld and further elaborated in the two other books referred to.

Apart from these three main books of *tafsīr*, numerous other attempts have been made to interpret the Qur'ān for the contemporary age. All efforts of *tafsīr* are however, apart

43 The last *juz'* of this book is now available in English: Qutb, Sayyid: *In the Shade of the Qur'ān* (Vol. 30), MWH Publishers, London, 1979.

44 See Ahmad, Khurshid: 'Some thoughts on a new Urdu tafsīr', in *Actes du XXIXe Congres International des Orientalistes,* I, I, Paris, 1975, pp.1-7.

45 English translation, so far nine volumes, up to *Sūra* 26, published under the title *The Meaning of the Qur'ān*, Islamic Publications Ltd., Lahore, 1967-79.

from their varying degrees of utility and reliability, only human efforts to present the Qur'ānic message in accordance with the needs and requirements of the age, and therefore in the final analysis can be only faint reflections of the Qur'ān as the word of God, against which all human efforts are inadequate, incomplete and of only limited validity. This basic principle, which all *mufassirūn* make the starting point of their work, should also be well remembered by the readers of the books of *tafsīr*, so as to remain aware of the actual book from Allah, the Qur'ān, upon which all exegesis and explanation rests.

TRANSLATION OF THE QUR'ĀN

By translation (*tarjama*) of the Qur'ān is meant the expression of the meaning of its text in a language different from the language of the Qur'ān, in order that those not familiar with it may know about it and understand Allah's guidance and will.

There is agreement among Muslim scholars that it is impossible to transfer the original Qur'ān word by word in an identical fashion into another language. This is due to several reasons:

— Words of different languages do not express all the shades of meanings of their counterparts, though they may express specific concepts.

— The narrowing down of the meaning of the Qur'ān to specific concepts in a foreign language would mean missing out other important dimensions.

— The presentation of the Qur'ān in a different language would therefore result in confusion and misguidance.

However, there is no doubt that translations of the meanings of the Qur'ān had already been made at the time of the Prophet Muḥammad as a solution for those who did not understand the language of the Qur'ān:

When Heraclius, the Byzantine emperor received the message Muḥammad had sent to him by messenger, the verses of the Qur'ān therein, together with the message, had to be translated, and the report by Abū Sufyān on this matter[46] states *expressis verbis* that translators were called for the conversation between the emperor and Abū Sufyān and that the message from the Prophet included a passage from the Qur'ān, namely *Sūra* 3: 64.

Similarly, translation from a passage from *Sūra Maryam* (19), which was recited by the Muslims in front of the Negus of Abyssinia[47] must have occurred. It might even be taken as indicating that the Muslims carried with them written extracts from the Qur'ān in case the Negas questioned them, before one of them recited from the Qur'ān: do you have something with you from what he brought from Allah?[48]

There is also some reference to the Persian language:

'Some Iranians – one is not certain whether they were from Yemen or Bahrain, Oman or elsewhere – were converted to Islam and applied for permission to say their prayers temporarily in their mother tongue. The Persian Salmān al Farisī translated the first chapter (*Sūra al-fātiḥa*) and sent it to one of them.'[49]

Translation of the Meanings

A word-by-word translation of the Qur'ān into another language would not be adequate. Therefore good translators have always aimed at first determining the meaning of a passage and then rendering it into the other language. Hence translations of the Qur'ān are actually expressions of meanings of the Qur'ān in other languages. M. Pickthall, one of the well-known English Qur'ān translators opened his Foreword with the following lines:

---

46 Bukhārī, VI, No. 75.

47 See Ibn Hishām, p.152.

48 *hal ma'aka mimā ja'a bihi 'an allāhi min shai'*: see Ibn Hishām, Arabic I, p.224.

49 Hamidullah, Munabbih, p.19; also: *Le Saint Coran,* p.xxxvi; see also: 'Is the Qur'ān translatable? Early Muslim Opinion', in: Tibawi, A. L., *Arabic and Islamic Themes*, Luzac, London, 1974, pp.72-85, here p.73.

'The aim of this work is to present to English readers what Muslims the world over hold to be the meaning of the words of the Qur'ān and the nature of that Book . . . The Qur'ān cannot be translated. That is the belief of old fashioned Sheikhs and the view of the present writer. The book is here rendered almost literally and every effort has been made to choose befitting language. But the result is not the glorious Qur'ān, that inimitable symphony the very sounds of which move men to tears and ecstasy. It is only an attempt to present the meaning of the Qur'ān – and peradventure something of the charm – in English.'[50]

Limitations of Translation

The Qur'ān is the word of Allah. Scholars say that since the Qur'ān has been revealed in the Arabic language any translation of it would not be the word of Allah. Furthermore, the concept of the uniqueness and inimitability of the Qur'ān (*i'jāz al-qur'ān*) is, in the mind of these scholars, closely linked to its expression in the Arabic language. This would become immaterial in translation. Lastly, because of the different meanings that words carry in different languages, the translation would never adequately express all the meanings of the Qur'ān carried by the original text.

Importance of Translations and their Benefits

The translations of the meanings of the Qur'ān are of great importance for two reasons:

— To present the message of Islam to non-Muslims and invite them to ponder over the Qur'ān.

— To point out to Muslims the revealed guidance and will of Allah to be observed by them.

Without translations of the Qur'ān today there is no way of effective *da'wa* either to non-Muslims or to Muslims them-

50 Pickthall, M. M.: *The Meaning of the Glorious Koran*, New York, 1963.

selves since those familiar with the language of the Qur'ān are few in number, and the vast majority of people have no opportunity to become acquainted with the meaning of the Qur'ān unless it be rendered into their mother tongue.

Translations of the meanings of the Qur'ān therefore are not only permissible but a duty and obligation upon Muslims,[51] and the practical basis for the extension of the Islamic *da'wa* to other peoples all over the world.

Translation in Ṣalāt?[52]

There is a difference of opinion as to whether the translated meanings of the Qur'ānic verse could be recited during prayer. Some scholars (in particular some Hanafites) say that someone not familiar with the Qur'ānic language may recite short passages in his mother tongue until he has learnt them in the Qur'ānic language.[53] The majority of scholars say that this would render the prayer invalid and only recitation of the Qur'ān in its revealed form is permissible.

Which Translation?

The first translation of the Qur'ān, from Arabic into Latin, made in Europe was done under the instructions of Peter the Venerable, Abbot of Cluny, in 1143. It was an attempt at the dawn of crusades and to equip the 'reconquerors' for mission among Muslims and refutation of Islam, and since then many other translations have followed.

Here we are however only concerned with translations into the English language. Borrowing from the field of *tafsīr* (and translation, as we have seen is certainly some kind of *tafsīr*, since the expression of its meaning in another language require *tafsīr*) the conditions which need to be fulfilled would be:

— The translation must be done by someone with the correct belief, i.e. by a Muslim.

---

51 Ṣābūnī, *tibyān*, p.232.
52 See Qaṭṭān, *op.cit.*, pp..272-6.
53 See also GdQ, III, p.106.

— The translation must be done by someone with adequate knowledge of both the language of the Qur'ān and the language for the translation.
— The translation must be done by someone well acquainted with the related sciences, such as *ḥadīth*, *tafsīr*, etc.

From the above principles it is obvious that all such translations by missionaries and their help-mates, the orientalists (even if excellent with regard to their English idiom)[54] should be rejected. This also applies to all non-Muslim translators and to those holding beliefs other than those based on the Qur'ān and *sunna*.

Authors well grounded in Islam but proposing explanations not in conformity with the consensus should be read with caution.

Translations by persons with insufficient knowledge of either language, or with insufficient educational background, poor knowledge of related sciences, etc., are of little use and may confuse, if not mispresent, the meanings of the Qur'ān.

There remain only a few translations into English which can be recommended. Among them the following two seem most useful:

— Abdullah Yusuf Ali: This is a book of mixed value, since the translation in places is a little far from the text. The numerous footnotes provide helpful explanations and background information but some of them seem odd if not unacceptable.
— Marmaduke Pickthall: This is a mere translation with no explanation and footnotes which makes it perhaps more difficult for the beginner. The author took great care to give as far as possible a literal translation.

54 Such as e.g. Arberry, A. J.: *The Koran Interpreted*, London, 1964.

CHAPTER 7

Some Related Issues

THE QUR'ĀN AS A MIRACLE

I'jāz al-Qur'ān

Why do we call the Qur'ān a miracle? The Qur'ān has certain features which make it unique and of inimitable quality. This inimitability is called *i'jāz al-qur'ān*, the 'miraculous nature' of the Qur'ān.

The word *i'jāz* is derived from the root *'ajaza'* which has various meanings, ranging from 'to be incapable, to make powerless', to 'to be impossible, to be inimitable'.

In technical language it means the inimitable and unique nature of the Qur'ān which leaves its opponents powerless or incapable of meeting the challenge which the revelation poses to them. It is also said that the Qur'ān is the *mu'jiza*, the miracle of Muḥammad:

> 'Narrated Abū Huraira: The Prophet said "Every prophet was given miracles because of which people believed but what I have been given is divine inspiration which Allah has revealed to me so I hope that my followers will outnumber the followers of the other prophets on the Day of Resurrection".'[1]

What is a Miracle?[2]

According to Muslim scholars the following five conditions

---

1 Bukhārī, VI, No. 504.
2 Ṣābūnī, *tibyān*, p.99.

must be met before an event can be accepted as a miracle from Allah:

— That no one else apart from Allah the Master of the world is able to do it.
— That it breaks the usual norms and differs from the laws of nature (not the laws of Allah, but the way nature normally is).
— That it serves as proof for the truth and claim of the messenger.
— That it happens in accordance with the messenger's claim.
— That the event happens through the messenger and no one else.

The Taḥaddī

Muḥammad was an unlettered man (*ummī*) but proclaimed a recited message. The challenge (*taḥaddī*) to others to imitate the Qur'ān has been posed by the revelation itself on various occasions and in various ways:

> 'Say: Then bring ye a book from God which is a better guide than either of them that I may follow it if ye are truthful' (28: 49).

However, the Qur'ān declares that no one could possibly bring such a book, not even if man and jinn combined their efforts (17: 90).

This challenge is repeated more than once: the enemies of the Prophet should produce ten *sūras* if their disbelief was justified (11: 16) or only one *sūra* (10: 39).

> 'If you are in doubt as to what We have revealed from time to time to Our servant, then produce a sūra like thereunto and call your witnesses or helpers besides God if your (doubts) are true but if ye cannot – and of surety you cannot – then fear the fire, whose fuel is men and stones – which is prepared for those who reject faith' (2: 23-4).

This challenge posed by the Qur'ān has never been met, precisely because of the reason the Qur'ān itself gives: that it cannot be done. If at any point in time, whether during the lifetime of the Prophet Muḥammad or at any other time someone had met this challenge, the opponents of Islam would certainly have made full use of it, but among the manifold attacks which have been, and are still being launched against Islam, none has been or is in this particular line. The *taḥaddī*, which has not been met and, as the Qur'ān says, cannot be met, is one of the main aspects of the unique and inimitable nature of the Qur'ān called *i'jāz*.

Various Aspects of I'jāz

The Muslim scholar al-Qurtubī (d.656/1258) in his commentary on the Qur'ān has indicated the following ten aspects of the *i'jāz al-qur'ān*:

— Its language excels all other Arabic language.
— Its style excels all other Arabic style.
— Its comprehensiveness cannot be matched.
— Its legislation cannot be surpassed.
— Its narrations about the unknown can only result from revelation.
— Its lack of contradiction with the sound natural sciences.
— Its fulfilment of all that it promises, both good tidings and threat.
— The knowledge it comprises (both legal and concerning the creation).
— Its fulfilment of human needs.
— Its effect on the hearts of men.

Others, such as al-Bāqillanī (d.403/1013) in his book *i'jāz al-qur'ān*[3] have discussed the following three aspects:

1 **The unlettered Prophet.** Prophet Muḥammad has been called '*ummī*', unlettered. Some say that Muḥammad could

3 Printed on the margin of Suyūṭī's *itqān*.

neither read nor write at all, but *ummī* may also mean that he belonged to an uneducated people. Perhaps he did read or write a little or perhaps not. This does not affect his basic situation as *ummī*. He was not a scholar and not a historian, neither was he a philosopher nor a priest and the common view is that he did not even read or write but he proclaimed the Qur'ān and recited its many *sūras* and *āyāt* in which he informed about the earlier prophets, earlier scriptures and earlier events, all in spite of his belonging to an uneducated people, in one of the most remote parts of the world and far away from the centres of civilisation and culture. In this also is one of the aspects of *i'jāz al-qur'ān*.

2 **The unseen world.** Another aspect of the *i'jāz al-qur'ān* are the prophesies it contains which are only possible with knowledge of the unseen world. The best-known such prophecy concerns the historical victory of the Romans over the Persians, shortly after the Romans had been defeated by the Persians and this prophecy was fulfilled during the Prophet's lifetime, when the enemies of Islam could themselves be witnesses to it:

> 'The Roman Empire has been defeated in a land close by; but they (even) after (this) defeat of theirs will soon be victorious within a few years' (30: 2-3).

The defeat of the Romans had taken place in 614/15, when Jerusalem was taken by the Persians, while the defeat of the Persians began only seven years later, when the Romans won the battle at Issus in 622.

Another prophecy is the victory of Islam over all other religions (9: 33; 24: 54).

3 **No contradictions.** The message of the Qur'ān revealed over a period of 23 years in both short and longer parts, on numerous occasions and in a variety of circumstances is nevertheless free of any contradictions. If the Qur'ān had been written by a human being then certainly some contradiction would be there and could be discerned. Already the Qur'ān has pointed out this fact:

'Do they not consider the Qur'ān? Had it been from other than God they would surely have found therein much discrepancy' (4:82).

The Literary Aspect

Scholars have also pointed out that there does not exist a piece of literature that can match the Qur'ān, with respect either to style and form or to content.

The Ṣarfa

Some mu'tazila have suggested that it should normally be possible to imitate the Qur'ān for there is nothing inimitable in it, but that it was Allah's 'aversion' (*ṣarfa*) which prevented the enemies of Islam from doing so.

Other scholars have disagreed with this, saying that this contradicts the view of holding the Qur'ān itself to be a miracle, while the 'aversion-view' suggests that the miracle lies in Allah's interference preventing the opponents of Islam from producing something like the Qur'ān.

The Qur'ān and a Computer Study

In *Sūra* 74:30 the following *āya* has sometimes perturbed the interpreters: 'Over it are 19'.

A computer study made in the U.S.A. by a Muslim scientist revealed that the figure 19 is of some significance to the composition of the text.[4]

The computer data reportedly revealed that the numbers of certain letters in various *sūras* are always multiples of 19, e.g. that the *Sūra qāf* contains the letter *qāf* 57 times which is a multiple of 19 (3 times 19), and that the formula *Bismillāh* is composed of 19 letters and that this formula occurs 114 times in the Qur'ān which is 19 times 6 (namely in front of each *sūra* except *Sūra* 9 (= 113) but one more time in *Sūra* 27:30 (= 113 plus 1)), and that each of the four words in the formula occurs in multiples of 19 in the Qur'ān etc. However, this latter claim

4 See Khalifa, R.: *The Perpetual Miracle of Muhammad*, Tucson, 1978; also Deedat, A.: *Al-Qur'ān the Ultimate Miracle*, Durban, 1979.

is not correct, as a simple count with the help of 'Abd al-Bāqī's concordance shows.[5]

From these findings the researcher has concluded that it is not humanly possible to compose a text of the size, form and content of the Qur'ān, with these underlying features. To him this is the 'mathematical proof' for the unique nature of the Qur'ān.

The Miracle of the Qur'ān

While there may be, and in fact is, some difference of opinion with regard to the relevance of all the indications given for the *i'jāz* of the Qur'ān including both the oldest classical scholars' views as well as the latest computer studies – the real unique feature of the Qur'ān is seen by all Muslims as being Allah's *guidance* for mankind, and there is no other and no better guidance than this. This makes the Qur'ān unique and inimitable. 'The miracle of the Qur'ān lies in its being the *hidāya* (guidance).' This is what is claimed by the Qur'ān, 'Say (unto them): Then bring a scripture (*kitāb*) from the presence of Allah that gives clearer guidance (*ahdā*) than those so (that) I may follow it, if you are truthful' (*al-qaṣaṣ* 28: 49). Here lies the uniqueness, miraculousness and supremacy of the Qur'ān over all other writings. Herein lies the miracle of the Qur'ān. The claim is evident. The content of the *hidāya* is evident. No single person, whether human or jinn, can produce a better *hidāya* than the Qur'ān . . . the Qur'ān, by claiming to be 'unique guidance' transcends all superficial characteristics assigned to it by a finite human mind. The message of the Qur'ān is extremely simple, remarkably clear: 'Anyone who will seek *hidāya* (guidance) with an open mind, a non-coloured vision and unbiased ears will reach the truth'.[6]

---

5 *al-mu'jam al-mufahras li-alfāẓ al-qur'ān al-karīm*, Cairo.

6 Ahmad, A.: 'The Miracle called Qur'ān at the mercy of Charlatans', in *Al-Ittihad*, April, 1978, pp.45-62, here 61-2. This article also contains a brief review of the classical views on *i'jāz*.

THE QUR'ĀN AND SCIENCE

Science could be broadly defined as knowledge – as far as it is available – about the material universe, described as accurately as possible. Scientific research is the attempt to obtain such knowledge, and a scientific truth or a scientific fact is the result of this research. Science as knowledge about things is also considered to be a branch of truth, but the important aspect of this is that scientific truths are not ultimate but change continuously. The continuousness of scientific research and discovery means that the scientific truth of today will be seen in a different light tomorrow, as new elements of knowledge become available. Lastly, being an endeavour of the human mind with all its faculties as well as limitations, scientific facts do constitute a *human* perspective with all its variety and limitations, on the true nature of things.

Science and the Qur'ān

The classical scholars while dealing with the unique nature of the Qur'ān (*i'jāz al-qur'ān*) had already pointed out that the Qur'ān contains information about the nature of things, the material environment, etc.[7] and that this information is not in conflict with man's perspective and experience. Furthermore, the development of science and its immediate effect upon the lives and societies of Muslims, especially during the last and in the present century, have led many Muslims to look at science against the background of the Qur'ān, and they have made numerous suggestions about the correct description in the Qur'ān of certain scientific facts.

Among some of the very important aspects of this line of thought, i.e. that the Qur'ān contains information on scientific facts which are in perfect agreement with the findings of man's scientific pursuits, are the following:[8]

7 See above, *i'jāz al-qur'ān*.

8 Bucaille's approach in his book *The Bible, the Qur'ān and Science*, Indianapolis, 1978, is more cautious. He writes: 'The Qur'ān did not contain a single statement that was assailable from the modern scientific point of view' (Introduction, p.viii).

— That the earth was previously part of the sun and only after separation from it became a habitable place for mankind (21:30).
— That all life originated from water (21:30).
— That the universe was in the shape of a fiery gas (which the Qur'ān calls *dukhān*) (41:11).
— That matter is made up of minute particles (10:62).
— That the oxygen content of the air is reduced at higher altitudes (6:125).
— That in nature everything consists of complementary elements, not only man and animals, but also plants and even inorganic matter (36:36).
— That the embryo in the womb is enclosed by three coverings (39:6).
— That fertilisation of certain plants is done by the wind (15:22).
— That microscopic organisms exist that are not visible to the naked eye, such as spermatozoon (96:1).
— That each human being has permanent individual fingerprints. (75:4).

These are just a few of many examples.[9]

All these matters which are in agreement with scientific findings could not, it is argued, have been known to any human being at the time of the revelation of the Qur'ān. They were only discovered many centuries later after intense scientific research. Hence their inclusion in the Qur'ān shows the heavenly origin of the book. This heavenly origin is further corroborated, the argument continues, by the correctness of the description of the scientific facts.

Science or the Qur'ān?

The basic question that needs to be raised here despite the

9 See Ṣābūnī, *tibyān*, pp.131-7; for more examples and detailed discussion, see also Bucaille, M., *op.cit.*

very attractive evidence presented by the scholars and writers from the field of science, is: If a scientific fact which is held to be valid, since it presents the latest result of scientific research, is in agreement with the Qur'ān today and if one is convinced solely by this argument of the heavenly origin of the Qur'ān, what will be one's attitude, when or if, after more intensive research, the very same scientific fact is seen in a new light and perhaps differs from what one previously accepted as the Qur'ān's position on the matter? Should this discrepancy then convince us of the human origin of the Qur'ān, and so refute its heavenly origin? In other words, until very recently, very many scientific facts were in utter disagreement with today's scientific truths – and if today's scientific truths are in agreement with the Qur'ān, this means that perhaps a few decades or a century ago no believer in science could have been convinced of the heavenly origin of the Qur'ān. Similarly, a few decades or a century from now, science, which is after all the human perspective on the true nature of things, might describe its findings entirely differently from the way it presents its 'truths' today.

Science and scientific truths, therefore, cannot be generally accepted as criteria for the genuineness or non-human origin of the Qur'ān, although at this point in time there are perhaps many good examples to be cited for the concordance between science and the Qur'ān on certain questions. However, the Qur'ān is a book of guidance for mankind and not a book of science nor a mine of cryptic notes on scientific facts.

Muslims believe the Qur'ān to be guidance from Allah, while science is a human endeavour and we believe the Qur'ān to be guidance from Allah under any circumstances irrespective of whether science, which changes continuously, seems to be in support of it or not.[10]

---

10 In my view, even Bucaille's attempt at qualification is unsatisfactory. Bucaille says he wishes to use 'data definitely established . . . incontrovertible facts and even if science can only provide incomplete data, they will nevertheless be sufficiently well-established to be used without fear of error' (Introduction, p.vii). His case in point is: 'It has been established that the earth revolves around the sun and the moon around the earth and this fact will not be subject to revision' (p.123). But it is precisely this point which led to the great Copernican controversy only a few centuries ago and previously it was as staunchly asserted that the sun revolves around the earth! What guarantee is there that no new perspective in science will completely

One of the main preoccupations of the few orientalists who have ever seriously studied the Qur'ān has been to investigate what they conceived to be the original order of the Qur'ānic text, since to them the 'chronological arrangement is of fundamental importance for the understanding of the text'.[11]

This effort resulted in a number of studies of the text of the Qur'ān as well as several translations of the Qur'ān with a 'rearrangement' of the *sūras*.[12]

Strangely enough, although during the past two centuries of more intense orientalist study of Islam perhaps tens of thousands of books on Islam have been written and published by the orientalists, the original studies on the Qur'ān, which are the sole basis of all research on Islam, number not more than half a dozen or so. For a quick overview follow brief reviews of the original works by orientalists on the Qur'ān – apart from translations – published during the present century.

Geschichte des Qorans.[13] This 'History of the Qur'ān' produced by four German orientalists, deals in three parts with 'The Origin of the Qur'ān', 'The Collection of the Qur'ān' and the 'History of the Qur'ānic Text'. The complete book naturally reflects the different approaches and types of scholarship of the various authors. Noldeke's bias against Islam can still be

---

note 10 continued
alter our present view? This is the best example to show that we should not accept scientific facts as absolute truths. They are rather what we presently know about them.

11 *Shorter Encyclopaedia of Islam*, Leiden, 1961, p.284.

12 All orientalists classified the *sūras* into several periods, some Makkan and some Madinan. The most original contribution here is Weil, G.: *Historisch-Kritische Einleitung in den Koran,* Bielefeld and Leipzig, 1878. See also Muir, W.: *The Coran, its composition and teaching*, London, 1878. and especially Noldeke, Th.: *Geschichte des Qorans,* upon which is based Rodwell, A.: *The Coran, translation with the Suras arranged in chronological order,* London, 1876. Other such rearranged translations are: Bell, R.: *The Quran translated with a critical rearrangement of the Suras*, Edinburgh, 1937 and Blachère, R.: *Le Coran. Traduction nouvelle,* Paris, 1949-50. Naturally the translations had to go even further in the attempt at 're-classification' by allotting a particular place to each verse and cannot restrict themselves to looking at *sūras* only.

13 Noldeke, T., et. al.: *Geschichte des Qorans*, Leipzig, 1909-38, in 3 parts.

clearly discerned, although he later renounced some of his views regarding the history of the Qur'ān.[14]

The main substance of the first volume is its second part 'On the Origin of the Various Parts of the Qur'ān'. Here, on the basis of Noldeke's earlier work, the *sūras* have been arranged in four periods, three Makkan and one Madinan, depending heavily on Muslim sources, especially on Suyūṭī's *itqān* and Ṭabarī. Due to this, the material presented is, apart from the usual biased comments, a good cross-section of classical Muslim writings on the subject. Incidentally, Pickthall (the well-known Qur'ān translator), relied heavily on this for his remarks on chronology in his translation.[15]

There is a final section on 'Revelation not included in the Qur'ān' discussed on the basis of various *aḥādīth* and other sources.

The second volume, dealing with the collection, is almost completely based on Muslim sources (again *itqān* dominates) and presents a calm discussion of the 'ruling tradition' *vis-à-vis* other reports about the collection of the Qur'ān. Schwally, after presenting the material and his reflection on it, comes to conclusions very close to the Muslim classical views, namely that 'the shape of the Qur'ān, as we have it now, was completed two to three years after the death of Muḥammad, since the 'Uthmānic edition is only a copy of Ḥafṣa's piece, the editorial work of which had been completed under Abū Bakr, or at latest under 'Umar. This editorial work however probably only concerned the compositions of the *sūras* and their arrangement. As far as the various pieces of revelation are concerned, we may be confident that their text has been generally transmitted exactly as it was found in the Prophet's legacy'.[16]

Volume three is mostly concerned with the written text of the Qur'ān and the various readings. It is once more a sober presentation of information derived basically from Muslim

---

14 See Part II, p.76 and his Preface to the 2nd edition, about his former view that the 'abbreviated letters' found at the beginning of certain *sūras* are the initials of the scribes or owners of the manuscripts.

15 See the various short introductions to the *sūras*, e.g. p.31, note 2; p.32, note 1; p.78, note 2; etc. in Pickthall, M. *op.cit.*

16 GdQ, II, p.120.

sources. Bergstraesser has dealt mainly with the written form of the 'Uthmānic Qur'ān, the variant readings, as contained in the *maṣāḥīf* of Ibn Mas'ūd and 'Ubay. He then introduces the historical development of the *qirā'a*.

Pretzl presents the various readings, emphasising the famous 'seven readings', describes the Muslim literature on *qirā'a* and finally deals very briefly with the palaeography and decorative designs of old Qur'ānic manuscripts. As in volume two, the main sources are classical Muslim authors, especially Suyūṭī Mabānī, Jazarī and various writers on *qirā'a*. Until today, Noldeke/Schwally is the most comprehensive – if not the sole – serious attempt by orientalists to deal with the Qur'ān – at least in a descriptive manner. For this is what the later authors – not so much Noldeke – had in view: to collect the available material on the subject and to present it. While some of the authors' comments and conclusions would not be welcomed by Muslims, the vast area that has been covered and the presentation based on the classical Muslim literature on the topic are of a merit that has to be acknowledged.[17]

Especially in the latter two volumes, there is surprisingly little that Muslims might find derogatory in style, and indeed the basic presentation is not unlike the classical Muslim literature on the subject.[18]

Materials for the History of the Text of the Qur'ān.[19] The author was one of the few orientalists, who concentrated at all

17 Hence it is not surprising to find that Yusuf Ali, the well-known translator of the Qur'ān into English, did not say more about this book (when he knew it, volume three was not even published) than simply: A German essay on the chronology of the Qur'ān. Its criticisms and conclusions are from a non-Muslim point of view and to us not always acceptable, though it is practically the last word of European scholarship on the subject'. *The Holy Qur'ān*, Lahore, 1934 (Introduction, p.xiv).

18 Blachère's *Introduction* (Blachère, R.: *Introduction au Coran,* Paris, 1947), to which Ṣāliḥ has often referred when refuting the orientalists' views, is not much more than a French summary of Noldeke-Schwally. Blachère freely admits that he owes much to them (p.XXIX), but seems to be less detached than his German predecessors. He often makes quite unfitting suggestions and raises questions attempting to cast doubt upon matters accepted among Muslims, and also not refuted by Noldeke-Schwally. In this he is closer to Noldeke's original work than the revised version of *Geschichte des Qorans*. Also, his constant reference to the 'Uthmānic text as the '*vulgate*' indicates how difficult it must be for him to look beyond the horizon of his Western-Christian tradition.

19 Jeffery, Arthur: *Materials for the History of the Text of the Qur'ān. The old codices.* Leiden, 1937.

seriously on the subject of Qur'ānic studies, and perhaps until very recently the only English-speaking scholar in this field. As the title suggests, this book was intended 'as a contribution to the problem of the history of the Qur'ān text' with the chief aim to finally 'write the history of the development of the *Qur'ānic* text'.[20]

Jeffery has combined in this volume the edition of an Arabic manuscript entitled *Kitāb al-maṣāḥif* by Ibn Abī Dāwūd (d.316/928) with a long list of so-called 'variant readings' of the Arabic text of the Qur'ān. By 'variant readings' are meant the differences between the Qur'ānic text as we have it today and the oldest sources about the written text of the Qur'ān. Such differences had occurred in the personally written collections of the Qur'ānic text, which some of the Companions of the Prophet and their followers had prepared for their personal use before the Caliph 'Uthmān had several copies of the Qur'ān prepared and sent to various Muslim regions.

Jeffery's suggestion is of course that the text of the Qur'ān, as we have it today, is not the 'original' or 'correct' version, but has been tampered with, if not by many hands, then at least by 'Uthmān and/or Abū Bakr, who were involved with the collection of the material of the Qur'ān. Only such an assumption could justify the objective of the orientalists to collect as much information on the 'pre-'Uthmānic codices' (i.e. written collections of the Qur'ān) in order to relate such information to the present text, and thus prepare a 'critical apparatus' as has been done, e.g., with the Bible. Nevertheless, this voluminous study appears to be a useful collection of information on such variant readings, from a total of 28 collections attributed to the Companions of the Prophet and their followers.

Jeffery's attempt to 're-construct' a critical text of the Qur'ān has apparently not been successful, since it was never published.[21]

Secondly, and this to me is of much greater importance: all the variants – or probably most of them – listed in the classical

20 *ibid.*, p.vii.

21 *ibid.*, p.17.

works from which Jeffery has drawn his information, must be supplied with an *isnād*, showing how the information about the particular variant reading has been obtained and transmitted. Perhaps Jeffery might have thought it useless to study the *isnād* – since orientalists usually assume that they are fabricated anyway. But if this is so, from where then does the confidence arise that his collection can be of any use for a critical text of the Qur'ān? However, in my view, the *isnād* needs to be scrutinised carefully in each and every case to see which of the reports on variant readings are indeed probable or improbable, and among the probable ones, which are sound and which are not. All this, it is true, can still be done, but Jeffery's collection is only of limited use for such a study.

The Collection of the Qur'ān. John Burton's book The Collection of the Qur'ān[22] is the latest attempt by a Western orientalist to rewrite the history of the Qur'ānic text. Burton attempts to cast doubt upon all the *aḥādīth* in connection with the history of the Qur'ānic text. He simply adopts the 'method' of Goldziher and Schacht, who have argued that many, if not all, *aḥādīth* are the result of second and third century forgery.[23]

In particular, Burton suggests that the legal scholars of the second/third century adopted some practices not based on the Qur'ān. In order to support these they invented the theory of *al nāsikh wa al-mansūkh*,[24] as well as the various reports about the collection of the Qur'ānic text. In particular they attributed a number of variant readings to several Companions of the Prophet, supposedly strengthening their argument.[25]

Their opponents, according to Burton, therefore invented the dominant version of the history of the collection of the Qur'ān at the time of 'Uthmān to strengthen their case.[26]

---

22 Cambridge University Press, Cambridge, 1977.

23 Introduction, pp.5-6.

24 Suggesting that such practices are based on verses of the revelation, the wording of which was abrogated but the legal ruling of which remained intact (*naskh al-tilāwa dūna al-ḥukm*), p.63.

25 p.44

26 pp.196-7.

All reports about the collection of the Qur'ān are therefore contradictory and inventions.[27]

At the end of his book, Burton maintains that the text of the Qur'ān we now have in our hands is 'the text which has come down to us in the form in which it was organised and approved by the Prophet. . . What we have today in our hands is the *muṣḥaf* of Muhammad'.[28]

Burton's account, though fascinating in its conclusions, is weak in several instances: The Goldziher-Schacht perspective has already been refuted.[29] Hence to adopt it and to apply it to the history of the Qur'ān cannot be convincing.

Burton's instances to prove that 'certain debated topics' among the legal scholars motivated the invention of reports and attribution of variant collections of the Qur'ān text to a number of Companions, are in fact only two.[30] This is not sufficient proof for such a grave accusation.

The collections of the Companions[31] which according to Burton were 'invented' together with their variant readings do *not* contain any such verses which could be used to support the legal views of some alleged parties. In fact, *none* of these Companions has either of the two verses (stoning verse, suckling verse) differing from 'Uthmān's text.[32]

Burton developed a new theory, based partly on his predecessors among the orientalists, but differing from their presentation and conclusions.[33] He failed to substantiate some

---

27 p.225.

28 pp.239-40.

29 In particular by scholars who proved that *aḥādīth* had been written down in the first century. To propose that they were fabricated in the second/third century means to reject this evidence (see, for example; Sezgin, Fuad: *Geschichte der Arabischen Literatur*, Leiden, 1967, Volume 1: Ḥamidullah, Muḥammad: *Saḥīfa Ibn Munabbih*, Paris, 1979).

30 The so-called 'verse of stoning' (p.72ff) and the so-called 'verse of suckling' (p.86ff).

31 Such as Ibn Mas'ūd and Ubay Ibn Ka'b.

32 See p.220 where Burton himself describes the actual differences between them and 'Uthmān's text.

33 A study of the book suggests also that his particular claim – to open new avenues because of access to several manuscripts not known to his predecessors – cannot be accepted. Although he cites seven manuscripts in his bibliography, none of them apparently features prominently in his presentation or documentation. Also Burton himself does not indicate *where* these manuscripts shed new light upon the subject and they rather seem to express what other sources also contained.

of the most important of his claims, such as e.g. that the 'collections' of the Companions were invented to support the legal usage concerning punishment of adultery or the practice of suckling, for none of these 'collections' by the Companions differ in these matters from the text of 'Uthmān, which is the Qur'ānic text we read today, and the text of the revelation Muḥammad proclaimed.

CHAPTER 8

Reading and Studying the Qur'ān

ETIQUETTE WITH THE QUR'ĀN[1]

Cleanliness

The Holy Qur'ān is the word of Allah addressed to us, and we should therefore treat it with due respect. One of the prime conditions for handling the Qur'ān has been set in the book itself:

> 'A book well guarded which none shall touch but those who are clean' (56: 78-9).

This means that in order to *touch* the Qur'ān one needs to be in a state of ritual purity (*ṭahāra*) to be obtained through *wuḍū'* or *ghusl*, as the case may be.[2]

The Right Niyya

When taking up the Qur'ān for study, recitation and reflection it must be done with the intention to seek Allah's pleasure. Although worldly gain may be found in the revelation from Allah, as may be derived from practices in religion and Islam, the true servant of Allah is concerned with the world to come and considers his actions here and now as preparation for the life to come.

In a *ḥadīth* reported by 'Ubaida al-Malikī the Prophet Muḥammad said:

---

1 See also the following paragraphs on 'Reciting the Qur'ān', 'Memorisation' and 'How to study the Qur'ān'.

2 As to *reciting* from the Qur'ān, (without touching it) there is indication from the *ḥadīth* that the Prophet recited with or without *wuḍū'*, but not in the state of impurity after sexual intercourse. Women also do not recite while menstruating.

'O ye who believe in the Qur'ān, do not make it a pillow, but correctly recite it day and night and popularise its recitation. Pronounce its words correctly and whatever is said in the Qur'ān you should think over it to take guidance from it that you may become successful and never think of gaining worldly benefits through it but recite it just to secure God's pleasure'.[3]

There are a number of points in this advice from the Prophet which we need to consider:

— Recite it day and night; this implies a *regularity* of Qur'ānic recitation which should be a continuous preoccupation.
— Popularise it; this implies that one should firstly observe the instruction to recite regularly and secondly *invite and give encouragement to others* to do so, such as one's family members, relatives, friends, etc.
— Pronounce its words correctly; this implies that one needs to pay attention to *correct pronunciation* both of the various letters as well as words, length, pauses, etc.
— Think over it; this implies the need to *understand* what one recites. Although mere recitation of words is also of some benefit, the Prophet's instruction is unmistakably clear that one should reflect, seek guidance and hence act upon what one recites. This is indeed a very important point, especially in the present state of Muslims, where hardly anyone reflects upon the Qur'ān and acts upon it.[4]

Of course the Prophet's emphasis on reflecting and acting is based upon Allah's instruction in the Holy Qur'ān itself:

'(Here is) a book which we have sent down unto thee, full of blessings, that they may meditate on its signs, and

---

3 Hashimi, R.: *A Guide to Moral Rectitude*, Delhi, 1972, pp.114-5.

4 For today many Muslims do not understand the Arabic of the Qur'ān, and even the average Arab of today has little access to the Qur'ānic language. Hence the great need to encourage all Muslims, especially the younger generation, to attempt to learn the language of the Qur'ān and to constantly refer to reliable translations of the Qur'ān in one's mother tongue as long as one has not yet progressed in Qur'ānic Arabic.

that men of understanding may receive admonition' (38:29).

— Recite (and reflect, seek guidance from and act upon) for the sake of Allah alone.

Etiquette of Reading and Reciting

— Keep the Qur'ān in a clean place.
— Seek only Allah's pleasure not any worldly gain.
— Concentrate fully and leave aside all other preoccupations.
— Be ritually clean, and sit on clean ground.
— Preferably sit facing the *qibla*.
— Ibn Mas'ūd read the Qur'ān in the mosque while kneeling on both knees.[5]
— Observe humility, tranquility and respect.
— Begin with *ta'awwudh* . . . and *basmala*.
— Read with a good voice.
— Ask Allah's blessing when reading a verse which contains a promise, and ask Allah's help when reading a verse which contains a threat.
— Repeat important verses many times.
— Say '*ṣadaqa-llāhu-l-'aẓīm*' at the end of the recitation, and close with a *du'ā'* that Allah may accept it from you.

Also:

— Let no day pass without reading the Qur'ān.
— Do not read in a manner that disturbs others.
— Sometimes read alone, sometimes in a group (your family too!).
— Reply, if someone gives *salām* while you read.
— Interrupt, when you hear the *adhān*.
— Observe *sajda al-tilāwa*.
— Memorise as much as you can.

5 Abū Dāwūd, see Kamāl, *op.cit.*, p.114.

Sajda al-Tilāwa

There are fourteen (or fifteen) *āyāt* in the Qur'ān, which require you to perform a prostration, when you read (or hear) these *āyāt*. In them it is mentioned that Allah's servants and creation bow before their Lord. These *ayāt* are the following: 7:206; 13:15; 16:49/50; 17:109; 19:58; 22:18; (22:77); 25:60; 27:25/26; 32:15; 38:24/25; 41:38; 53:62; 84:20/21; 96:19.

The *sajda al-tilāwa* is performed as follows:

— Form *niyya*.
— Face the *qibla* (standing or sitting).
— Say *takbīr*.
— Touch the ground in prostration with toes, knees, palms, nose and forehead.
— While in *sajda* recite any words to glorify Allah, such as: *subḥāna rabbi-al-a'lā,* or other similar words.
— Rise, saying *takbīr*.

Prostration for recitation (*sajda al-tilāwa*) is not a new practice but has been ordered and observed by the Prophet Muḥammad himself:

> Ibn 'Umar reported: The messenger of Allah while reciting the Qur'ān recited its sura containing sajda, and he performed prostration and we also prostrated along with him (but we were so overcrowded) that some of us could not find a place for our forehead (when prostrating ourselves).[6]

RECITING THE QUR'ĀN[7]

The very first revelation to the Prophet Muḥammad instructs him to recite the Qur'ān:

---

6 *Ṣaḥīḥ* Muslim, I, p.287, No. 1189.

7 Suyūṭī, *itqān*, I, p.99ff; for an interesting background study of historical development and 'musical' aspects see Farūqī, in *Islamic Perspectives*, *op.cit.*, pp.105-19.

> 'Read, in the name of thy Lord . . .' (96: 1),

and soon afterwards in *Sūra al-muzzammil* he is told to observe a particular manner of recitation, which has since become the common form among Muslims of reading the Qur'ān:

> 'And recite the Qur'ān in slow, measured rhythmic tones' (73: 4).

This manner of reading (*tilāwa*) the Qur'ān is achieved by observing the rules of *tajwīd*.

The word *tajwīd* is derived from the Arabic root '*jawwada*', which means 'to make well', or 'to improve'. It means 'making good'. In technical language it carries two distinct meanings:

— Correct and good pronunciation in recitation.
— A mode of recitation of medium speed.

Tajwīd and Qirā'a

The knowledge of recitation (*'ilm al-qirā'a*), includes three main branches, one of which is *tajwīd*:

— Knowledge about *tajwīd,* i.e. correct and good pronunciation.
— Knowledge about the various readings (see under *qirā'a*).
— Knowledge about the various modes of recitation, among them:
  — *ḥadr*, i.e. at normal talking speed.
  — *tartīl*, i.e. slow, for reading and reflection.
  — *tajwīd taḥqīq*, i.e. like *tartīl*, but with greatest care, for the purpose of teaching and learning.
  — *tajwīd* (also known as *tadwīr*), between *ḥadr* and *tartīl*.

The Importance of Tajwīd

Since *tajwīd* is a basic part of the knowledge of *qirā'a*, its importance is obvious. One of its great advantages is that proper knowledge about *tajwīd* – which is not difficult to acquire – will lead to the correct recitation of the Qur'ān, irrespective of whether one knows the language of the Qur'ān or not.

Basic Rules

Basically, *'ilm al-tajwīd*, the knowledge about *tajwīd*, is of two branches:

— The correct pronunciation of various letters in different places.

— The correct length and emphasis given to the vowels under different circumstances.

An outline of the main principles is given below:

Nūn Sākin and Tanwīn. The letter *nūn* ن with *sukūn* نْ is called *nūn sākin* e.g. in the word *min* مِنْ, while the symbols for *an* ً , *in* ٍ *un* ٌ are called *tanwīn*, as e.g. in the word *ghafūrun* غَفُوْرٌ

Full Assimilation. When either of the two letters *ra* ر or *lam* ل follow *nūn sākin* or *tanwīn*, there occurs full assimilation (*idghām*) of the n-sound to the letter after it, e.g.: (*mir-rabbihim*) مِنْ رَّبِّهِمْ (*wa lam yakun lahu kufuwan aḥad*)

وَلَمْ يَكُنْ لَّهُ كُفُواً اَحَدٌ

Nasal Assimilation. When one of the letters *yā* ي, *nūn* ن, *mīm* م, *wāw* و, follow a *nūn sākin* or *tanwīn*, there occurs assimilation with nasalisation (*idghām bi-ghunna*) of the n-sound to the letter after it, e.g.:

(*man-ya'mal*) ي مَنْ يَّعْمَلْ

(*yauma idhin-nā'imatun*) ن يَوْمَئِذٍ نَّاعِمَةٌ

(*rasūlun-min qablī*) م رَسُوْلٌ مِّنْ قَبْلِي

(*raḥīmun-wadūd*) و رَحِيْمٌ وَّدُوْدٌ

There are four exceptions to this rule, where the *nūn sākin* occurs within the word: صِنْوَانٌ قِنْوَانٌ دُنْيَا بُنْيَانٌ

Substitution. The n-sound of *nūn sākin* or *tanwīn*, followed by the letter *bā* is substituted (*iqlāb*) by m, e.g.: (*samīʿum-baṣīr*) سَمِيْعٌ بَصِيْرٌ

All other letters, following *nūn sākin* or *tanwīn*, do not modify and are not modified, but are clearly pronounced (*iẓhār*).

Mīm Sākin. The letter *mīm* م with *sukūn* مْ is called *mīm sākin* as e.g. in the word هُمْ
When followed by either the letter *bā* ب or *mīm* م, assimilation to the m-sound takes place, as e.g.:

(*wa mā hum-bi muʾminīn*)	ب	وَمَا هُمْ بِمُؤْمِنِيْنَ
(*in kuntum-muʾminīn*)	م	إِنْ كُنْتُمْ مُؤْمِنِيْنَ

Intensification. The following five letters when with *sukūn*, require some intensification (*qalqala*) in pronunciation: *qāf* ق *ṭā* ط *dāl* د *jīm* ج *bā* ب, e.g.:

(*subḥāna llāh*)	ب	سُبْحَانَ اللّٰه
(*kharajnā*)	ج	خَرَجْنَا
(*al-qadr*)	د	الْقَدْرُ
(*fiṭratun*)	ط	فِطْرَةٌ
(*khalaqnā*)	ق	خَلَقْنَا

(There is no *qalqala* for *dāl* with *sukūn*, if followed by the letter *ṭā* ط or *tā* ت.)

Slight Assimilation. *Nūn sākin* or *tanwīn*, followed by one of the 15 letters given below is concealed (*ikhfāʾ*) by slight assimilation, e.g.:

kuntum	ت	كُنْتُمْ
min thamarāt	ث	مِنْ ثَمَراتٍ
in jāʾakum	ج	إِنْ جَاءَكُمْ
ʿindahum	د	عِنْدَهُمْ

min dhikri	ن	مِنْ ذِكْرٍ
yanza'u	ز	يَنْزَعُ
qaulan sadīdan	س	قَوْلاً سَدِيْداً
min sha'ā'iri llāh	ش	مِنْ شَعَائِرِ اللّٰهِ
yanṣūru	ص	يَنْصُرُ
manḍūd	ض	مَنْضُوْدٍ
kalimatin tayyibatin	ط	كَلِمَةٍ طَيِّبَةٍ
yanẓurūna	ظ	يَنْظُرُوْنَ
infirū	ف	اَنْفِرُوا
min qablihim	ق	مِنْ قَبْلِهِمْ
man kāna	ك	مَنْ كَانَ

Further Assimilations. Assimilation of the first to the second letter also occurs, as in the examples given below, when the first letter is with *sukūn*:

qad tabayyana	ت	د	قَد تَّبَيَّنَ
athqalat da'awā	د	ت	أَثْقَلَت دَّعَوَا
hammat ṭā'ifa	ط	ت	هَمَّت طَّائِفَةٌ
idh ẓalamtum	ظ	ذ	إِذ ظَّلَمْتُم
yalhath dhālik	ذ	ث	يَلْهَث ذَّلِك
nakhluqkum	ك	ق	نَخْلُقكُّم
qul-rabbi	ر	ل	قُلْ رَبِّ

The Letter Lām. The letter *lām* ل will be pronounced lightly, when preceded by a letter with *kasra* e.g. *bismi-llāh* بِسْمِ اللّٰه.

It will be pronounced strongly, when preceded by a letter with *fatḥa* or *dhamma*, e.g. *qul huwa-llāhu aḥad* قُلْ هُوَ اللّٰهُ اَحَدٌ

The Letter Rā. The letter *rā* ر will be pronounced lightly in connection with the i-sound, i.e. when preceded by a letter with *kasra* or by *yā sākina*: يْ or itself carries a *kasra*, with or without *tashdīd*, e.g.:

abṣir أَبْصِر

khabīr خَبِيْر

rizq رِزْق

min sharri مِنْ شَرِّ

It is pronounced strongly in connection with the a- and u-sounds, i.e. when it carries *fatḥa* or *dhamma* with or without *tashdīd*, or carries *sukūn*:

arāda llahu أَرادَ اللّهُ

barqun بَرْقٌ

laisa-l-birra لَيْسَ الْبِرَّ

Prolongation. The three vowels *alif* ا *wāw* و *yā* ي have different prolongation (*madd*) in different places. The measure of prolongation is called 'one *alif*', which is the normal length of pronouncing *alif*.

Natural Prolongation (*madd ṭab'ī*). The vowel is read at the length of two *alifs*, e.g.: *māliki yaumi-dīn* مٰلِكِ يَوْمِ الدِّين

Prolongation against Sukūn (*madd 'āriḍ li-sukūn*). This occurs when the vowel is the second last letter of a word, and one wishes to pause after this particular word. In such a case prolongation of the length of two or more *alifs* is required, e.g.:

wa llāhu 'alīmun-bi-ẓẓālimīn وَاللّهُ عَلِيْمٌ بِالظّالِمِيْنَ

Prolongation of Hamza (*madd al-hamz*). There are two kinds of such prolongations. The first one occurs when a word ends with a vowel and the following word begins with *hamza*. The required length of the vowel sound would be two to six *alifs*, e.g.

wa idhā aradnā وَإذا أَرَدْنا

The other case is the *hamza* within a word after a vowel, e.g.:

al-malā'ika الْمَلآئِكَةُ

Compulsory Prolongation (*madd lāzim*). This is prolongation of any vowel followed by a letter with *sukūn* or *tashdīd*. Its length would be two *alifs*. e.g.:

qāf wa-l-qur'āni-l-majīd ق وَالقُرْآنِ الْمَجِيْدِ

al-ḥāqqa الْحَاقَّةُ

Reading Signs in the Text. Most copies of the printed Qur'ān have a number of additional signs, which help, in addition to the rules of *tajwīd*, with correct recitation. The two most important of these are:

lām alif لا meaning no stop allowed, and

mīm م meaning stop compulsory.

The meaning of these symbols are as follows:

Stop

ο end of an *āya*

م *waqf lāzim,* compulsory stop; reading on will change meaning e.g. in *Sūra* 2: 8-9:

'But they do not (really) believe. Fain would they deceive God. . .'

Without stop this would suggest that the believers deceive God.

قف *qif*, pause.

Stop Preferred

ط | *waqf muṭlaq,* at the end of a sentence or though

ج | *waqf jā'iz,* permissible, recommended stop.

Pause

سكته or س *sakta* short pause, without taking breath.

وقفه longer pause, without taking breath.

No Stop

لا *lā yūqafu* – in the middle of the line, i.e. no stop, at the end of an *āya*, i.e. optional no stop.

No Stop Preferred

ز *waqf mujawwaz*

صلى *ṣali,* connect.

ص *waqf murakhkhaṣ;* permissible stop, if taking breath is required.

After such a stop repetition from a previous stop is required.

Other Signs

ك *kadhālik*, as before, i.e. observe here as the previous sign.

ق *qad qīla*, it has been said (to stop) optional.

قلا *qīla lā*, it has been said not to (stop); optional.

معانقه or مع observe either first or second sign only as e.g. in *Sūra* 2: 2.

صلى where more than one sign occurs,
ج usually the topmost one is preferred.

وقف الغفران *waqf al-ghufrān;* said to be meritous to stop here.

وقف المنزل *waqf al-manzil* or
وقف جبرئيل *waqf jibrīl*; where the Angel Gabriel is said to have stopped.

وقف النبي *waqf al-nabī*; where the Prophet is said to have stopped.

ع *rukū*'.

حزب *ḥizb* (see under 'Divisions of the Text'.)

جزء *juz'*.

منزل *manzil.*

سجدة *sajda* (see under 'Etiquette with the Qur'ān'.)

MEMORISATION OF THE QUR'ĀN

Memorisation (*ḥifẓ, taḥfīẓ)* of the Qur'ān was the earliest form of transmission of the text[8] and has been practised by Muslims since the revelation began. The Qur'ān is perhaps the only book in human history that has such an outstanding tradition of oral transmission which can be traced back to the Prophet Muḥammad himself. Although many Muslims known as *ḥāfiẓ* (pl. *ḥuffāẓ*) have memorised the complete Qur'ān, it is an obligation for each Muslim to memorise as much of it as he is capable of doing. It is reported from Ibn 'Abbās that Allah's messenger said:

> 'He in whose heart there is no part of the Qur'ān is like unto a deserted house'.[9]

While in the past memorisation of the Qur'ān used to be the basis of all sound Muslim education, today there is less emphasis on it due to changes in the educational system of the Muslims. However, memorisation of passages from the Qur'ān is still required from all Muslims particularly because of the following reasons:

— Memorisation was the *sunna* of the Prophet and observed by the Companions and *tabi'ūn* and all pious Muslims.

— Recitation of passages from memory is required for the correct performance of prayer.

— Passages memorised are useful in practical *da'wa* work.

— Memorisation and repetition of the Qur'ān leads to more remembrance and awareness of Allah and His message.

— Memorisation of the *aḥkām* passages leads to more consciousness and determination.

— Memorisation leads to a deeper understanding of and deeper faith in the message of the Qur'ān.

8 See above.

9 Tirmidhī, in: Kandahlavi, M.Z., *Virtues of the Holy Qur'ān*, Multan, 1968, No. 15.

How to Memorise Passages from the Qur'ān

The following practical suggestions are aimed at helping you to memorise more passages from the Holy Qur'ān:

— Make memorisation a part of your daily routine. Do a little at a time but do it regularly.
— Choose a passage which is particularly meaningful to you. It should not be very long.
— Read this passage aloud a few times.
— Write this passage on a small piece of paper.
— Memorise it.
— Read it from memory.
— Ask someone to read it for you from the *muṣḥaf*.
— Write down what he has read.
— Recite the portion in your prayers.
— After you have memorised the passage, repeat it on many occasions (such as during prayer, etc.) which will deeply engrave it into your memory ('overlearning').
— Choose another passage and do likewise.

THE QUR'ĀN ON RECORDS, TAPES AND CASSETTES

Aids for the Layman

While the Qur'ān has been somewhat standardised in practical terms, as far as the writing is concerned, through the distribution of printed copies, the recited Qur'ān has had to face, through the advancement of technology, a similar development. Recordings of the recited Qur'ān in passages have been made since the 1920s. Today both recording and replay equipment are much more advanced. Replay devices (gramophones, recorders) are widespread. More important even, radio broadcasts have reached virtually every corner of the world, and the recited Qur'ān, often from recordings and not always in a live broadcast, reaches many ears and minds.

Indeed today students are able to memorise passages from the Qur'ān using recordings. The benefit for the untrained is obvious: the recited Qur'ān is available anywhere, anytime, without the physical presence of a *ḥāfiẓ*.

Problems for the Scholar

Along with the benefit for the untrained goes a particular problem: the Qur'ān is available in a number of ways of recitation (the seven *aḥruf*) but of course a recording can present only *one* of the several accepted readings.

The reading presently available in recorded versions is the one by Ḥafṣ, which therefore has become extremely popular and widespread, while other readings, such as the North African style, (Warsh) are – at least in the public consciousness – pushed somewhat into the background.

In Egypt a plan has been developed to record the recitation of the Qur'ān also in the other accepted readings. It is not known how far this has been implemented.[10]

Well-Known Reciters

Presently there are a number of recitations of the Qur'ān available on cassette tapes, the better known among them being:

— Shaikh 'Abdullāh al-Khayyāṭ, 22 cassettes (very fast speed).

— Shaikh Maḥmūd Khalīl, al-Ḥuṣarī, 22 cassettes (medium speed, good for learning).

— Shaikh 'Abd al-Bāsiṭ 'Abd al-Ṣamad, 44 cassettes (slow speed).

There are numerous other Qur'ān readers available on cassettes, not only from the Middle East but from all over the Muslim world.

The best-known lady reader seems to be Nūr Asiah Djamīl from Indonesia.

---

10 See Sa'īd Labīb: *al-muṣḥaf al-murattal*, Cairo, 1967; partly translated into English: Berger, M., Rauf, A., Weiss, B.: *The Recorded Qur'ān*, Princeton, 1974.

Qur'ān Reading Competitions

Events, where several readers participate, take place all over the Muslim world. These have been specially popularised in Malaysia, where it has been an annual event in *ramaḍān* since 1961 to invite the best local readers and readers from other countries to recite in public. While the idea of competition or contest is unsuitable to the recitation of the Qur'ān, the programme does help to some extent to popularise the recitation of the Qur'ān.

Recent attempts in Saudi Arabia to offer cash prizes for the memorisation and recitation of the Qur'ān must be seen as one of the more unfortunate attempts to cope with a serious decline in the art of recitation, probably due to the Westernisation of educational systems all over the Muslim world, in which the memorisation and recital of the Qur'ān is no longer considered important.

HOW TO STUDY THE QUR'ĀN

The demands which the Qur'ān puts on every Muslim are summarised as follows:[11]

— A Muslim is required to believe in the Qur'ān.
— He is required to read it.
— He is required to understand it.
— He is required to act upon its teachings.
— He is required to convey its teachings to others.

It is obvious that perhaps only one of these five obligations could be fulfilled without understanding the Qur'ān, and proper understanding of it is derived from its study.

Read and Reflect

The Qur'ān itself emphasises that mere reading or reciting

11 See Ahmad, Israr: *The Obligations Muslims Owe to the Qur'ān*. Markazi Anjuman Khuddam-ul-quran, Lahore, 1979, p.5.

of it is insufficient. To do justice to the Qur'ān one needs to reflect upon what one reads, and then act upon it:

> '(Here is) a Book which We have sent down unto thee, full of blessings, that they may meditate on its signs, and that men of understanding may receive admonition' (38:29).
>
> 'Do they not then earnestly seek to understand the Qur'ān or are their hearts locked up by them?' (47:24; see also 4:82; 23:68).

Similarly the Prophet instructed Muslims to recite the Qur'ān as well as to reflect upon it:

> 'O ye who believe in the Qur'ān, do not make it a pillow, but correctly recite it day and night and popularise its recitation. Pronounce its words correctly and whatever is said in the Qur'ān you should think over it to take guidance from it that you may become successful and never think of gaining worldly benefits through it but recite it just to secure God's pleasure'.[12]

What Approach?

To derive a proper understanding of the Qur'ān from your study, you need to adopt the correct approach. A clear outline of how the Qur'ān should be approached for reflection and study has been given by K. Murad. His essay on *The Way to the Qur'ān*[13] is most commendable. A brief outline of its main features is given below:

Observe the basic prerequisites for the fruitful study of the Qur'ān:

— Be fully convinced that it is Allah's revelation.
— Read it to seek the pleasure of Allah alone.
— Accept its guidance fully and completely.
— Mould yourself according to its guidance.

---

12 Hashimi, R.: *A Guide to Moral Rectitude*, Delhi, 1972, pp.114-5.
13 Published together with the Qur'ān translation by A. Y. Ali, Leicester, 1978.

— Seek refuge with Allah, seek His help for the study, and praise and glorify Him for His blessings through the Qur'ān.

Strengthen and maintain the 'presence of the heart':

— Be aware that you are always in Allah's presence.
— Feel, as though you hear the Qur'ān from Allah.
— Feel, as though the Qur'ān addresses you directly.
— Observe the proper outward posture, and purify yourself inwardly and outwardly.

Reflect over the Qur'ān and strive to understand it:

— Consider each *āya* as relevant today, not as a thing of the past.
— Read the whole of the Qur'ān (using a translation if necessary) for an overview.
— Avoid lengthy commentaries in the beginning of your study.
— Learn the language of the Qur'ān.
— Reflect deeply upon what you read, and recite in a slow harmonious mode (*tartīl*).

Strive for full inner participation in your study:

— Remember how the Prophet and his Companions reacted to the Qur'ān.
— Take each passage of the revelation as addressed to you.
— Develop an inner response to the *āyāt,* and express it by praising Allah, seeking His forgiveness, etc.

Strive to live by the teachings of the Qur'ān, since it is Allah's guidance for mankind. This is the way to get close to the Qur'ān and to grasp its meanings. To know about the Qur'ān in application, observe in everyday life the way of the Prophet Muḥammad, who was described by 'Ā'isha, his wife, as 'the living Qur'ān'. Also recite the Qur'ān daily and memorise what you can.

Some useful hints for the study of the Qur'ān have also been given by Abul A'la Mawdūdī[14] for those who seek guidance from the Book of Allah:

— Read the Qur'ān with a mind free from bias and preconceived ideas, as otherwise you will read your own notions into the book.
— Read the book more than once to get a sound insight.
— Note down whatever questions arise, while you read and note down their answers, which you will come across in other passages of the Qur'ān as you read on.
— Investigate in particular, while you read, which way of life the Qur'ān suggests to you.
— Undertake more detailed studies after such introductory readings, and inquire about the various aspects of Islam and how it ought to be applied.
— Do not forget that the real key to understanding the Qur'ān is the practical application of its meaning.

'. . . in spite of all these devices, one cannot grasp the inspiring spirit of the Qur'ān, unless one practically starts the work for the accomplishment of the mission for which it was revealed . . . One cannot possibly grasp the truths contained in the Qur'ān by the mere recitation of its words. For this purpose one must take active part in the conflict between belief and unbelief, Islam and un-Islam, truth and falsehood'.[15]

14 See 'Suggestions for Study', in Ali, A. Y., *The Holy Qur'ān*, Leicester, 1978, pp.xxi-xliii.
15 *ibid.*, p.xlii.

Select Bibliography

'ABD AL-BĀQĪ, Muḥammad Fu'ād, *al-mu'jam al-mufahras li alfāẓ al-qur'ān al-karīm*. Kitāb al-sha'b, Cairo, n.d.

ABBOTT, Nabia, *The Rise of the North-Arabic Script and its Koranic Development*. University of Chicago Press, Chicago, 1939.

——, *Studies in Arabic Literary Papyri, II: Qur'ānic Commentary and Tradition*. University of Chicago Press, Chicago, 1967.

AḤMAD, Anis, 'The Miracle Called Qur'ān at the Mercy of Charlatans', in: *Al-Ittiḥad* 15(2), 1978, 45-62.

AḤMAD, Isrār, *The Obligations Muslims Owe to the Qur'ān*. Anjuman Khuddām al-Qur'ān, Lahore, 1979.

AḤMAD, Khurshid (ed.), *The Holy Qur'ān: An Introduction*. Jami'at-ul-Falaḥ Publications, Karachi, 1387 (1967).

——, 'Some Thoughts on a New Urdu Tafsīr', in: *Actes du XXIXe Congrès International des Orientalistes. Etudes Arabes et Islamiques*. I – Histoire et Civilisation. L'Asiatheque, Paris, I, 1-7.

AḤMAD, Khurshid and ANṢĀRI, Zafar Isḥāq (eds.), *Islamic Perspectives: Studies in Honour of Mawlana Sayyid Abul A'la Mawdūdī*. The Islamic Foundation, Leicester, 1979.

AḤMAD, Ziāuddin, 'The Science of Quranic Exegesis', in: *The Islamic Literature*, 319-23.

AḤSAN, M. M., 'The Qur'ān and the Orientalists. A note on the authenticity of the so-called Satanic verses'. *The Islamic Quarterly* 24 (1980), 89-95.

ALAM, Tombak, *Ilmu Tajwid Populer*. Ghalia, Indonesia, Jakarta, 1978.

'ALAVI, Muḥammad Badruddin, 'Collection and Arrangement of the Qur'ān, in: *The Islamic Literature*, 341-54, 381-90.

'ALI, 'Abdullāh Yusuf, *The Glorious Qur'ān: Translation and Commentary*. The Islamic Foundation, Leicester, 1978.

'ALI, Mawlāna Moḥammad, *The Religion of Islam*. Aḥmadiya Anjuman Isha'at Islam, Lahore, 1936.

ANṢĀRĪ, Ibrāhīm b. 'Abdullāh, *Irshād al-hairān li ma'rifat āya al qur'ān*. Matābi' 'al-qatar al-waṭaniyya, qatar, 1400/1980.

ANṢĀRI, Muḥammad Fazl-ur-Raḥmān, *The Quranic Foundations and Structure of Muslim Society*. 2 vols. The World Federation of Islamic Missions, Karachi, 1973.

ARBERRY, Arthur J., *The Koran Interpreted*. Oxford University Press, London, 1964.

ASAD, Muḥammad, *The Message of the Qur'ān*. Brill, Leiden, London, 1979.

'AṬṬAR, Dawud, *Mūjaz 'ulūm al-qur'ān*. Mu'assasa al-'alā li-l-maṭbu'āt, Beirut, 1399/1979.

A'ẒAMI, M. M., *Kuttāb al-nabī*, Al-maktab al-Islāmī, Beirut, 1393/1974.

——, *Studies in Ḥadith Methodology and Literature*. American Trust Publications, Indianapolis, 1977.

BALJON, J. M. S., *Modern Muslim Koran Interpretation (1880-1960)*. Brill, Leiden, 1968.

BAQILLĀNĪ, 'On the Miraculous Nature (I'jāz) of the Qur'ān. From al-Baqillānī, I'jāz al-Qur'ān, in: JEFFERY, Arthur (ed.), *Islam, Muḥammad and His Religion*, op. cit.

BECK, Edmund, 'Die b. Mas'ūdvarianten bei al-Farrā', in: *Orientalia* 25 (1956), 353 ff.

BEESTON, A. F. L., *Baiḍāwī's Commentary on Surah 12 of the Qur'ān*. Oxford University Press, Oxford, 1963.

BELL, Richard, *The Qur'ān translated with a critical rearrangement of the Surahs*. Edinburgh University Press, Edinburgh, 1937.

BELL, William Y., *The Mutawakkil of al-Suyūṭi*. (Ph.D. Thesis), Yale, 1924.

BEN-NABI, Malek, *Le Phenomène Coranique. Essai d'une théorie sur le Coran*. Association des Etudiants Islamiques en France, Paris, 1976.

BINT AL-SHĀṬI', *al-qur'ān wa al-tafsīr al-'aṣrī*. Dar al-Ma'ārif, Cairo, 1970.

BISHOP, Eric F. F., *The Light of Inspiration and Secret Interpretation*, being a translation of the chapter of Joseph, Surah Yusuf, with the commentary of Naṣir al-Din al-Baiḍāwi. Jackson, Glasgow, 1957.

BLACHÈRE, Regis, *Introduction au Coran*. Maisonneuve, Paris, 1947.

——, *Le Coran. Traduction Nouvelle*. Paris, 1949-50.

BOULLATA, Issa J., 'Modern Qur'ān Exegesis. A Study of Bint al-Shāṭi's Method'. *The Muslim World* 64 (1974), 103-13.

BUCAILLE, Maurice, *The Bible, the Qur'ān and Science*. North American Trust Publications, Indianapolis, 1978.

BUKHĀRĪ, *Ṣaḥīḥ al-Bukhārī*. 9 vols. in 3. Cairo, 1313/1895.

BURTON, John, *Al-nāsikh wa al-mansūkh*. (Ph.D. Thesis), London, 1969.

—, *The Collection of the Qur'ān*. Cambridge University Press, Cambridge, 1977.

DAMAGHĀNĪ, Ḥussain b. Muḥammad, *Qāmūs al-qur'ān*. Dar al-'ilm li-l-mal'īn, Beirut (1400)/1980.

DARĀZ, Muḥammad 'Abdullāh, *Mādkhal ilā al-qur'ān al-karīm*. Dār al-Qur'ān al-Karīm, Kuwait, (1391)/1971.

DEEDAT, Ahmed, *Al-Qur'ān: The Ultimate Miracle*. The Islamic Propagation Centre, Durban, 1979.

DODGE, Bayard, *The Fihrist of al-Nadīm: A Tenth Century Survey of Muslim Culture*. 2 vols. Columbia University Press, New York, 1970.

DOI, A, Rahman I., *Introduction to the Qur'ān*. Islamic Publications Bureau, Lagos, 1976.

FĀRŪQĪ, Lāmyā', 'Tartīl al-Qur'ān al-Karīm', in: AḤMAD, Khurshid and Zafar Isḥāq ANṢĀRI, op. cit., 105-19.

FLÜGEL, Gustavus, *Corani texti Arabicus; Concordantiae Corani Arabicae*, Brett, Leipzig, 1834, 1898.

GÄTJE, Helmut, *The Qur'ān and its Exegesis*. Selected texts with classical and modern Muslim interpretations. Routledge & Kegan Paul, London, 1976.

GOLDZIHER, Ignaz, *Die Richtungen der Islamischen Koranauslegung*. Brill, Leiden, 1970.

GROHMANN, Adolf, *'Die Entstehung des Koran und die ältesten Koran-Handschriften'*, *Bustan*, 1961, 33-8.

GUILLAUME, E., *The Life of Muhammad*. Oxford University Press, London, 1955.

ḤAMĪDULLĀH, Muḥammad, *Le Saint Coran. Traduction Intégrale et Notes*. Club Francais du Livre, Paris, 1963.

———, *Ṣaḥifa Ḥammām Ibn Munabbih. The earliest extant work on the Hadith*. Centre Cultural Islamique, Paris, 1979.

———, 'Orthographical Peculiarities in the Text of the Qur'ān. A Guide on how to read it correctly'. *Islamic Order* 3 (1981), 71-86.

ḤAQQĀNI, Muḥammad 'Abdul Ḥaqq, *An Introduction to the Commentary on the Holy Qur'ān*, being an English translation of al-Bayan. Oriental Reprints, Lahore, 1975 (first 1910).

HASHIMI, Raḥīm 'Ali, *A Guide to Moral Rectitude*. Board of Islamic Publications, Delhi, 1972.

HUGHES, Thomas Patrick, *A Dictionary of Islam*. W. H. Allen, London, 1895.

IBN 'ABBĀS, *Tanwīr al-miqbās min tafsīr Ibn 'Abbās*. Dar al-Kutub al-'Ilmiyya, Beirut, (1360/1941).

IBN HISHĀM, *Sīra al-nabī*. 4 vols. Cairo, n.d.

IBN AL-JAUZĪ, *Tafsīr Ibn al-Jauzī (Zād al-masīr fī 'ilm al-tafsīr)*. 9 vols. Al-maktab al-islāmī, Beirut, 1384/1964.

IBN KATHĪR, *Tafsīr al-qur'ān al-'aẓīm*. 4 vols. Ḥalabī, Cairo, n.d.

———, *Mukhtaṣar tafsīr Ibn Kathīr*. 3 vols. Beirut: Dar al-qur'ān al-Karīm, 1402/1981.

IBN KHALDŪN, *Muqaddima*. Dar al-muṣḥaf, Cairo, n.d.

———, *The Muqaddimah*, transl. by F. Rosenthal. 3 vols. Princeton University Press, Princeton, 1967.

IBN SA'D, *Al-ṭabaqāt al-kubrā*. 9 vols. Dar al-taḥrīr, Cairo, n.d.

IBN SALĀMA, *Al-nāsikh wa al-mansūkh*. Cairo, Ḥalabī, 1387/1967.

IBN TAIMĪYA, *Muqaddima fī uṣūl al-tafsīr*. Dar al-qur'ān al-karīm, Kuwait, (1391)/1971.

IBRĀHĪM, Izzudin and Denis JOHNSON-DAVIS, *Forty Ḥadith Qudsi*. Holy Qur'ān Publishing House, Beirut, 1980.

Index cum Concordance for the Holy Qur'ān. The Holy Qur'ān Society of Pakistan, Karachi, 1974.

IRVING, T. B., 'Terms and Concepts: Problems in Translating the Qur'ān', in: AḤMAD, Khurshid and Zafar Isḥāq ANṢĀRI, op. cit., 121-34.

ISRAEL, Fred L. (ed.), *Major Peace Treaties of Modern History*. Chelsea House Publishers, New York.

JANSEN, J. J. G., *The Interpretation of the Qur'ān in Modern Egypt*. Brill, Leiden, 1974.

JEFFERY, Arthur, 'The Mystic Letters of the Koran', in: *The Moslem World* 14 (1924), 247-60.

———, *Materials for the history of the text of the Qur'ān (incl. kitāb al-maṣāḥif* by Ibn Abī Dāwūd). Brill, Leiden, 1937.

———, *The Foreign Vocabulary of the Qur'ān*. The Oriental Institute, Baroda, 1938.

———, 'The Textual History of the Qur'ān', in: *Journal of the Middle East Society* 1 (1947), 35-49.

———, *Islam, Muḥammad and His Religion*. Bobbs-Merrie, New York, 1958.

JOMIER, Jacques, *Le commentaire Coranique du Manar: tendences modernes de l'éxegèse coranique en Egypte*. Maisonneuve, Paris, 1954.

JULLANDRI, R., 'Qur'ānic exegesis and classical tafsīr', in: *The Islamic Quarterly*, London XII (1968), 71-119.

KAMĀL, Aḥmad 'Adil, *'Ulūm al-qur'ān*. Al-mukhtār al-islāmī, Cairo, 1394/1974.

KANDAHLAVĪ, Moḥammad Zakariyā, *Virtues of the Holy Qur'ān*. Nāzim Kutubkhanah, Multan, 1968.

KHADDURI, Majid, *Islamic Jurisprudence: Shafi'i's risala*. Johns Hopkins Press, Baltimore, 1961.

KHALĪFA, Rashād, *The Perpetual Miracle of Muhammad*. Tucson.

KHĀN, M. Ajmal, 'An Inquiry into the Earliest Collection of the Qur'ān', in: *Studies in Islam* 1 (1964), 175-212.

KHĀN, Muḥammad Muḥsin, *The Translation of the Meaning of Ṣaḥīḥ al-Bukhārī*. 9 vols. Ozkan, Istanbul, 1978.

LANE, Edward William, *Selection from the Kuran . . . with an interwoven commentary*. Madden, London, 1843.

LINGS, Martin and Yasin Ḥāmid SAFADI, *The Qur'ān*. The British Library Board, London, 1976.

MAḤALLĪ, Jalāl al-Dīn and Jalāl al-Dīn al-SUYŪṬĪ, *Tafsīr al-Jalālain*. Kitāb al-Sha'b, Cairo, 1390/1970.

MAKHDŪM, Ismā'īl, *Tarīkh al-muṣḥaf al-'uthmānī fī tashqand*. Al-Idāra al-dinīya, Tashkent 1391/1971.

MARGOLIOUTH, D. S., *Chrestomathia Baidawiana; the commentary of el-Baidawi on Sura III translated and explained*. Luzac, London, 1894.

MAWDŪDĪ, 'Abul A'lā, *The Meaning of the Qur'ān*. 9 vols. Islamic Publications, Lahore, 1967-1979.

———, *Introduction to the Study of the Qur'ān*. Jamā'at-i-Islami Hind, Delhi, 1971.

MENDELSOHN, Isaac, 'The Columbia University Copy of the Samarqand Kufic Qur'ān', in: *The Moslem World* 30 (1940), 375-8.

MUḤAISIN, Muḥammad Sālim, *Al-mustanīr fī takhrīj al-qira'āt al-mutawātira*. 3 vols. Maktab Jumhuriyya Miṣr, Cairo, 1396/1976.

MUIR, William, *The Coran. Its composition and teaching; and the testimony it bears to the Holy Scripture*. Society for the Promotion of Christian Knowledge, London, 1878.

———, *The Life of Mohammad from Original Sources* (Introduction). Edinburgh, 1923.

MUJĀHID, Abū al-Hajjāj, *Tafsīr Mujāhid*. 2 vols. Al-manshurāt al-'ilmiyya, Beirut, n.d.

Mu'jam alfāẓ al-qur'ān al-karīm, Dār al-Shurūq, Cairo, 1401/1981.

MUSLIM, *Ṣaḥīḥ Muslim bi-sharḥ al-Nawawī*. 18 vols. in 6. Cairo, 1384/1964.

NAḤḤĀS and IBN SALĀMA, 'Abrogation'. From al-Nahhas and Ibn Salāma . . . , in: JEFFERY, Arthur (ed.), *Islam, Muḥammad and His Religion*, op. cit.

NAWAWĪ, Muḥyī al-Dīn, *al-adhkār*. Ḥalabī, Cairo, 1375/1955.

NĪSĀBŪRĪ, 'On the eternal nature of the Word of Allah'. From an-Naisaburi's Gharā'ib al-Qur'ān, in: JEFFERY, Arthur (ed.), *Islam, Muhammad and His Religion*, op. cit.

NÖLDEKE, Th. et. al., *Geschichte des Qorans*. 3 vols. Dieterich'sche Verlagsbuchhandlung, Leipzig, 1909-38.

NOLIN, Kenneth, *The Itqān and its Sources*. (Ph.D. Thesis), Hartford, 1968.

NŪRI, K. R., *The Running Commentary of the Holy Qur'ān*. Sufi Hamsaya, Shillong (East Pakistan), 1964.

PACHOLCZYK, J. M., *Regulative principles in the Koran chant of Shaikh Abdul Basit Abdussamad*. (Diss.) Los Angeles, 1970.

PENRICE, John, *A Dictionary and Glossary of the Koran*. Curzon Press, London, 1979, (first 1873).

PICKTHALL, Mohammad Marmaduke, *The meaning of the Glorious Koran*. Mentor Books, New York, 1963.

QĀSIMĪ, 'On Reading or Reciting the Qur'ān'. From al-Qasimi's Maw'izat al-Mu'min . . . , in: JEFFERY, Arthur (ed.), *Islam, Muḥammad and His Religion*, op. cit.

QAṬṬĀN, Mānna', *Mabāḥith fī 'ulūm al-qur'ān*. Dar al-Sa'udīya li-al-nashr, Riyāḍh, 1391/1971.

QUASSEM, Muḥammad 'Abdul, *The Recitation and Interpretation of the Qur'ān. Al-Ghazālī's Theory*. The author, Kuala Lumpur, 1979.

QUṬB, Sayīd, *Fī ẓilāl al-qur'ān*. 6 vols. Dar al-shurūq, Beirut, (1393) 1973.

———, *In the Shade of the Qur'ān*, (extracts). The Islamic Study Circle, Loughborough, n.d. (cyclostyled).

———, *In the Shade of the Qur'ān*, Vol. 30. MWH Publishers, London, 1979.

RĀGHIB AL-ISFAHĀNĪ, *Al-mufradāt fī gharīb al-qur'ān*. Dar al-Ma'rifa, Beirut, n.d.

RAḤIMUDDĪN, Muḥammad, *Muwaṭṭa' Imām Mālik*. Ashraf, Lahore, 1980.

RAŪF, M. and B. WEISS, *The Recorded Qur'ān*. Darwin Press, Princeton, 1974.

RIḌĀ, Muḥammad Rashīd, *Tafsīr al-qur'ān al-ḥakīm*. 12 vols. Dār al-Ma'rifa, Beirut, n.d. (first 1354/1935).

ROBSON, James, *Mishkāt al-Maṣabīḥ*, (English translation). 4 vols. Ashraf, Lahore, 1963.

RODWELL, A., *The Coran, translation with the Surahs arranged in chronological order*. London, 1876.

RODWELL, J. M., *The Koran: Translated from the Arabic*. Everyman's Library, London, 1971.

ṢĀBŪNĪ, Muḥammad 'Alī, *Al-tibyān fī 'ulūm al-qur'ān*. Dār al-Irshād, Beirut 1390/1970.

———, *Ṣafwa al-tafāsīr*. 3 vols. Dar al-Qur'ān al-Karīm, Beirut, 1402/1981.

SA'ĪD, Labīb, *Al-muṣḥaf al-murratal*. Dār al-kitāb al-'Arabī, Cairo, (1387)/1967.

———, *The Recited Koran*. A history of the first recorded version. The Darwin Press, Princeton, 1975.

ṢALĀḤI, 'Adil, 'Recitation and Memorisation of the Qur'ān', in: *The Muslim* 3/4. 1976, 84-7.

SĀLIḤ, Ṣubḥī, *Mabāḥith fī 'ulūm al-qur'ān*. Dār al-'ilm li-l-maliyin, Beirut, (1384)/1964.

ṢAQR, 'Abd al-Badī', *al-tajwīd wa 'ulūm al-qur'ān*. Maktab Wahba, Cairo 1396/ (1976).

SARTAIN, E. M., *Jalal al-Din al-Suyuti*. Vol. 1: Biography and Background. Cambridge University Press, Cambridge, 1975.

ṢAWWĀF, Mujahid Muḥammad, 'Early Tafsīr – A Survey of Quranic Commentary up to 150 AH', in: AḤMAD, Khurshid and Zafar Isḥāq ANṢĀRI, op. cit., 135-45.

SEEMAN, Khalīl, *Ash-Shafi'i's Risala: Basic Ideas*. Ashraf, Lahore, 1961.

SELL, *The Faith of Islam*. Appendix A: 'Ilmu't-tajwid. Madras, 1907.

SEZGIN, Fuat, *Geschichte des Arabischen Schrifttums*. Vol. 1. Brill, Leiden, 1967.

SHĀFI'Ī, Muḥammad b. Idrīs, *Kitāb al-risāla*. Cairo, n.d.

SHĀH, Aḥmad Rev., *Miftāḥ-ul-Quran. Concordance and complete glossary of the Holy Qur'ān*. 2 vols. The Book House, Lahore, n.d. (first publ. 1906).

Shorter Encyclopaedia of Islam. Brill, Leiden, 1961.

SIDDIQUI, 'Abdul Ḥamīd, *Ṣaḥīḥ Muslim . . . rendered into English*. 4 vols. Ashraf, Lahore, 1978.

SIJISTĀNĪ, Abū Bakr, *Tafsīr gharīb al-qur'ān*. Maktaba 'alam al-fikr, Cairo, 1401/1980.

SUYŪṬĪ, Jalāl al-Dīn, *History of the Caliphs*, transl. by H. S. Jarrett. Baptist Mission Press, Calcutta, 1881.

———, *al-Itqān fī 'ulūm al-qur'ān*. 2 vols. in 1. Maktab al-thaqāfiyya, Beirut, 1393/1973.

———, *Lubāb al-nuqūl fī asbāb al-nuzūl*. Dār al-Tūnisīya li-al-nashr, Tunis, 1402/1981.

SYAMSU, Nazwar, *Kamus/Dictionary al-Qur'ān. Indonesian-English*, Ghalia, Indonesia, Jakarta, 1977.

ṬABARĪ, Muḥammad b. Jarīr, *Jāmi' al-bayān 'an ta'wīl āyāt al-qur'ān*. 30 vols. in 12. Ḥalabī, Cairo, 1398/1968.

TIBAWĪ, Abd al Latif, 'Is the Qur'ān Translatable? Early Muslim Opinion', in: *Arabic and Islamic Themes*. Luzac, London, 1974.

ṬUFAIL, Muḥammad, S., *The Qur'ān Reader*. An elementary course in reading the Arabic script of the Qur'ān. San Fernando (Trinidad), 1974.

TUJĪBĪ, Abū Yaḥyā, *Mukhtaṣar min tafsīr al-imām al-Ṭabarī*, 2 vols. al-hay'a al-misriyya, Cairo, 1390/1970.

WĀḤIDĪ, al-Nisābūrī, *Aṣbāb al-nuzūl*, Ḥalabī, Cairo, 1387/1968.

WANSBROUGH, J., *Quranic Studies: Sources and methods of scriptural interpretation*. Oxford University Press, Oxford, 1977.

WATT, W. Montgomery, *Bell's Introduction to the Qur'ān*. Edinburgh University Press, Edinburgh,1977.

WEIL, Gustav, *Historisch-Kritische Einleitung in den Koran*. Bielefeld und Leipzig, 1878.

WEISS, Bernard, 'Al-Muṣḥaf al-Murattal: A modern phonographic 'Collection' (Jam') of the Qur'ān', in: *The Muslim World* 64 (1974), 134-40.

WHERRY, E. M., *A Comprehensive Commentary on the Qur'ān*. London, 1882-86.

ZAMAKHSHARĪ, Muḥammad b. 'Umar, *al-Kashshāf*. 4 vols. Ḥalabī, Cairo, 1392/1972.

ZARKASHĪ, Badr al-Dīn, *al-burhān fī 'ulūm al-qur'ān*. 4 vols. Ḥalabī, Cairo, 1376/1958.

ZARQĀNĪ, Muḥammad A., *Manāhil al-'irfān fī 'ulūm al-qur'ān*. 2 vols. Ḥalabī, Cairo, (1362/1943).

Supplementary Select Bibliography

ABDUL-FATTAH, Ashraf (et al.), *Tajwīd-ul-Qur'ān: A New Approach to Mastering the Art of Reciting the Holy Qur'ān*. Bakkah Translation and Publishing Ltd., London, 1989.

ABU-LAYLA, Muhammad, 'The Qur'ān: Nature, Authenticity, Authority and Influence on the Muslim Mind'. *The Islamic Quarterly* (London) 36, 4 (1992), 227-41.

ADAMS, Charles J., 'Qur'ān: The Text and its History'. In: *The Encyclopaedia of Religion*. Macmillan, London, 1987, 156-76.

———, 'Abul A'lā Mawdūdī's *Tafhīm al-Qur'ān*'. In: Andrew Rippin (ed.), *Approaches to the History of the Interpretation of the Qur'ān*. Clarendon Press, Oxford, 1988, 307-24.

ADIL, Hafiz Muhammad, *Introduction to Qur'ān* (2nd Edition). Adam Publishers & Distributors, New Delhi, India, 1990.

AHMAD, Mulla Shamsuddin, *Al-Qur'ān and Modern Science*. Islam Prachar Samity, Dhaka, 1992.

AHMAD, Ziauddin, *Al-Qur'ān: Divine Book of Eternal Value*. Royal Book Company, Karachi, 1989.

AHMED, Hasanuddin, 'Qur'ānic Words of Non-Arabic Origin'. *Islamic Order*, 10, 1 (1988), 105-16.

———, *An Easy Way to the Understanding of the Qur'ān* (Parts I and II). Iqra' International Educational Foundation, Chicago, 1987.

AHMED, Qadeeruddin, 'Conservative and Liberal Understanding of the Qur'ān'. In: H.M. Said (ed.), *Essays on Islam*. Hamdard Foundation, Karachi, 1993, 32-49.

AHSAN, M.M., 'Believers and the Qur'ān: A Survey of Studies in English' (review article). *Muslim World Book Review* (Leicester) 7, 4 (Summer 1987), 3-20.

ALI, Ahmad (tr.), *Al-Qur'ān: A Contemporary Arabic and English Edition*. Oxford University Press, Delhi, 1987.

ALI, Salah Salim, 'Misrepresentation of Some Ellipted Structures in the Translation of the Qur'ān by A.Y. Ali and M.M. Pickthall'. *The Islamic Quarterly* (London), 35, 1 (1991), 48-54.

ALI, Syed Anwar, *Qur'ān: The Fundamental Law of Human Life, Vols. IV and V*. Hamdard Foundation Press, Karachi, 1987.

ANSARI, Iqbal Husain, *Corrections of Errors in Pickthall's English Translation of The Glorious Qur'ān, The Scripture Whereof there is no Doubt*. Iqbal Husain Ansari, Karachi, 1991.

ANSARI, Muhammad Baqir, 'Tahrif al-Qur'ān: A Study of Misconceptions Regarding Corruption of the Qur'ānic Text'. *Al-Tawhid* (Tehran), 4, 4 (1987), 11-23.

ANSARI, Zafar Afaq (ed.), *Qur'ānic Concepts of Human Psyche*. International Institute of Islamic Thought, Islamabad, 1992.

ARAFAT, Q. (comp.), *Incorrect Equivalents Chosen by Yusuf Ali in His Translation of the Qur'ān*. Arafat Islamic Publications, Leicester, 1991.

———, *The Qur'ān: The Conclusive Word of God*. Arafat Islamic Publications, Leicester, 1991.

ASKARI, Hasan, *Qur'ānic Discourse: Selected Readings*. Seven Mirrors Publishing House, Pudsey, UK, 1993.

AYOUB, Mahmoud, *The Qur'ān and Its Interpreters, Vol. 2: The House of 'Imrān*. State University of New York Press, Albany, New York, 1992.

BALJON, J.M.S., 'Qur'ānic Anthropomorphisms'. *Islamic Studies* (Islamabad), 27, 2 (1988), 129-50.

BENABOUD, Muhammad, 'Orientalism on the Revelation of the Prophet: The Cases of W. Montgomery Watt, Maxime Rodinson and Duncan Black MacDonald'. *The American Journal of Islamic Social Sciences*, 3, 2 (1986), 309-26.

BOSWORTH, C.E. and RICHARDSON, M.E.J. (eds.), *A Commentary on the Qur'ān*, Vol. 1: *Sūrahs I-XXIV;* Vol. 2: *Sūrahs XXV-CXIV*. University of Manchester, 1991.

BOULLATA, Issa J., 'The Rhetorical Interpretation of the Qur'ān: I'jaz and Related Topics'. In: Andrew Rippin (ed.), *Approaches to the History of the Interpretation of the Qur'ān*. Clarendon Press, Oxford, 1988, 139-57.

BURTON, J. (ed.), *Abū 'Ubaid Al-Qāsim b. Sallām's Kitāb Al-Nāsikh wa-l-Mansūkh* (Gibb Memorial Series, N.S., XXX). Gibb Memorial Trust, Cambridge, 1987.

———, 'Qur'ānic Exegesis'. In: M.J.L. Young (et al.) (eds.), *Religion, Learning and Science in the Abbasid Period*. Cambridge University Press, 1990.

CALDER, Norman, 'Tafsīr from Ṭabarī to Ibn Kathīr: Problems in the Description of a Genre, Illustrated with Reference to the Story of Abraham'. In G.R. Hawting and A.K.A. Shareef (eds.), *Approaches to the Qur'ān*. Routledge, London, 1993, 101-40.

'The Caliph Othman Koran' (Earliest Mushaf in Samarkand). *Religiya V SSR* (Moscow), No. 5 (1989), 18-21.

CHAWLA, La'l Muhammad, *A Study of Al-Qur'ān-ul-Karīm: Complete Arabic Text, English Translation, Synopses of Sūrahs and Explanatory Notes*. Islamic Publications, Lahore, 1991.

CRAGG, Kenneth (ed.), *Readings in the Qur'ān*. Collins, London, 1988.

FARUQI, I.H. Azad, *Tarjuman Al-Koran: A Critical Analysis of Maulana Abul Kalam Azad's Approach to the Understanding of the Koran*. Vikas Publishing House Ltd., New Delhi, 1991.

FEDERSPIEL, Howard M., 'An Introduction to Qur'ānic Commentaries in Contemporary Southeast Asia'. *The Muslim World* (Hartford), 81, 2 (1991), 149-65.

FITZGERALD, Michael L., 'Shi'ite Understanding of the Qur'ān'. *Encounter* (Rome), (October 1991), 3-12.

GOLDFELD, Y., 'The Development of Theory on Qur'ānic Exegesis in Islamic Scholarship'. *Studia Islamica* (Paris), 67 (1988), 5-27.

GREIFENHAGEN, F.V., 'Traduttore Tradirtore: An Analysis of the History of English Translations of the Qur'ān'. *Islam and Christian-Muslim Relations* (Birmingham), 3, 2 (1992), 274-91.

HABIL, Abdurrahman, 'Traditional Esoteric Commentaries on the Qur'ān'. In: Seyyed Hossein Nasr (ed.), *Islamic Spirituality: Foundations*. Routledge & Kegan Paul, London, 1987, 24-47.

HAERI, Shaykh Fadhlalla, *Heart of the Qur'ān and Perfect Mizan: Sūrat Yā Sīn*. Zahra Publications, Blanco, Texas, 1986.

———, *Man in the Qur'ān and the Meaning of Furqan: Sūrat al-Baqarah*. Zahra Publications, Blanco, Texas, 1986.

———, *The Light of Iman from the House of 'Imrān: Sūrat Āl 'Imrān*. Kegan Paul International, London, 1987.

———, *Keys to the Qur'ān, Volumes 1–5*. Garnet Publishing, Reading, UK, 1993.

———, *The Journey of the Universe as Expounded in the Qur'ān*. Routledge & Kegan Paul, London, 1987.

HALEEM, Muhammad Abdel, 'The Hereafter and Here-and-Now in the Qur'ān'. *The Islamic Quarterly* (London), 33, 2 (1989), 118-31.

HAMID, Saiyid, 'Conservatism and Liberalism in the Understanding of the Qur'ān'. *Hamdard Islamicus* (Karachi), 13, 3 (1990), 37-54.

HAMIDULLAH, Muhammad, 'Suggestions on Punctuation in the Copies of the Holy Qur'ān'. *Islamic Order* 8, 3 (1986), 17-24.

HAMMAD, Ahmad Zaki, 'Reflections on The Fairest of Stories: The Revelation of ''Joseph'' Interpreted in Context'. *Islamic Horizon* (Plainfield, USA), 18, 5-6 (1989), 25-53.

HANEEF, Iman Torres AL-, *The Qur'ān in Plain English for Children and Young People, Part 30 (Sūrahs 78-114)*. The Islamic Foundation, Leicester, 1993.

HASAN, Suhaib, *An Introduction to the Qur'ān* (Understanding Islam, Series 4). Al-Quran Society, London, 1989.

HAWTING, G.R. and SHAREEF, Abdul-Kader A. (eds.), *Approaches to the Qur'ān*. Routledge, London, 1993.

HUSAINI, Muhammad Zahid, *Commentators of the Holy Qur'ān (Tadhkirat al-Mufassirin)*. Ferozsons, Lahore, 1992.

IRVING, T.B. (et al.), *The Qur'ān: Basic Teachings* (Revised Edition). The Islamic Foundation, Leicester, 1992.

———, *The Noble Qur'ān, Arabic Text and English Translation*. Majdalawi Educational Institute, Amman, 1992.

JA'FARIYAN, Rasul, 'A Study in Sunni and Shi'i Traditions Concerning Tahrif'. *Al-Tawhid* (Tehran), Part 1: 6, 4 (1989), 19-50; Part 2: 7, 1 (1989), 33-52; Part 3: 7, 2 (1990), 15-38.

JAFRI, S. Husain M., 'Particularity and Universality of the Qur'ān with Special Reference to the Term Taqwa'. In: H.M. Said (ed.), *Essays on Islam*. Hamdard Foundation, Karachi, 1993, 14-31.

KHALIFA, Mohammad, *The Sublime Qur'ān and Orientalism*. International Islamic Publishers Ltd., Karachi, 1989.

KHALIL, Imaduddin, 'The Qur'ān and Modern Science: Observations on Methodology'. *The American Journal of Islamic Social Sciences* (Herndon), 8, 1 (1991), 1-13.

KHATIB, M.M., *The Bounteous Koran* (The Royal Cairo text in Arabic and English). Macmillan, London, 1986.

KHERIE, Al-Haj Khan Bahadur Altaf Ahmad, *A Key to the Holy Qur'ān: Index – Cum – Concordance for the Holy Qur'ān* (Reprint). Adam Publishers & Distributors, New Delhi, 1992.

KIDWAI, A.R., 'Translating the Untranslatable: A Survey of English Translations of the Qur'ān' (review article). *Muslim World Book Review* (Leicester), 7, 4 (Summer 1987), 66-71.

———, 'Arberry's "The Koran Interpreted": A Note'. *Hamdard Islamicus* (Karachi), 11, 3 (1988), 77-87.

KINBERG, L., 'Muḥkamāt And Mutashābihāt (Koran 3/7): Implication of a Koranic Pair of Terms in Medieval Exegesis'. *Arabica (Revue D'Etude Arabes),* (Leiden), 35, 2 (1988), 143-72.

LEEMHUIS, Fred, 'Origins and Early Development of the Tafsīr Tradition'. In: Andrew Rippin (ed.), *Approaches to the History of Interpretation of the Qur'ān*. Clarendon Press, Oxford, 1988, 13-30.

LINGS, Martin, *The Qur'ānic Art of Calligraphy and Illumination*. Interlink Books, New York, 1987.

LUKE, K., 'Similitudes and Parables in the Koran'. *Indian Theological Studies* 23, 1 (1986), 37-50.

McAULIFFE, Jane Dammen, *Qur'ānic Christians: An Analysis of Classical and Modern Exegesis*. Cambridge University Press, 1991.

MANZOOR, S. Parvez, 'Method Against Truth: Orientalism and Qur'ānic Studies' (review article). *Muslim World Book Review* (Leicester), 7, 4 (Summer 1987), 33-48.

MAQSOOD, Ruqaiyyah Waris, *The Koran* (Discovering Sacred Texts Series). Heinemann Educational, Oxford, 1993.

MAWDŪDĪ, Abul A'lā. *Towards Understanding the Qur'ān* (Tr. Zafar Ishaq Ansari), Vol.1: Sūrahs 1-3, 1988, 396; Vol.2: Sūrahs 4-6, 1989, 368; Vol.3: Sūrahs 7-9, 1990, 344; Vol.4: Sūrahs 10-16, 1993, 424. The Islamic Foundation, Leicester.

MIR, Mustansir, *Coherence in the Qur'ān*. American Trust Publications, Indianapolis, 1986.

———, *Verbal Idioms of the Qur'ān* (Michigan Series on the Middle East No.1). University of Michigan, Ann Arbor, 1989.

———, 'The Qur'ānic Oaths: Farahi's Interpretation'. *Islamic Studies* (Islamabad), 29, 1 (1990), 5-28.

MIRZA, Khan Zaman, 'The Qur'ānic Concept of History'. *Hamdard Islamicus* (Karachi), 13, 2 (1990), 11-34.

NADVI, M. Raziul Islam, 'Ayat (Signs): A Study in Qur'ānic Perspective'. *MAAS Journal of Islamic Science* (Aligarh), 7, 2 (1991), 19-44.

NADWI, Abdullah Abbas, *Learn the Language of the Holy Qur'ān* (Iqra' Programme of Arabic and Qur'ānic Studies). Iqra' International Education Foundation, Chicago, 1987.

NAYED, Aref Ali, 'The Radical Qur'ānic Hermeneutics of Sayyid Qutb'. *Islamic Studies* (Islamabad), 31, 3 (1992), 355-63.

NELSON, Kristine, *The Art of Reciting the Qur'ān*. University of Texas Press, Austin, 1986.

NIKITIN, Archimandrite Augustin, 'The Qur'ān of 'Uthmān' (The Oldest Mushaf). *Encounter* (Rome), 156-7 (June-July 1989), 3-8.

OZEK, Ali (et al.), *The Holy Qur'ān with English Translation*. Ilmi Nesriyat, Istanbul, 1992.

PHILIPS, Abu Ameenah Bilal, *Tafseer of Soorah Al-Hujuraat*. International Islamic Publishing House, Riyadh, 1988.

POWERS, David S., 'The Exegetical Genre Nasikh al-Qur'ān wa Mansukhuhu'. In: Andrew Rippin (ed.), *Approaches to the History of the Interpretation of the Qur'ān*. Clarendon Press, Oxford, 1988, 117-38.

QURESHI, M.M. Bhutta and JAFAR, S.M., *Qur'ānic Āyāt Containing Reference to Science and Technology*. Pakistan Science Foundation, Islamabad, 1987.

RAB, Syed Fazle (ed.), *The Qur'ān and the Contemporary Challenges*. Commonwealth Publishers, New Delhi, 1992.

RAFAI, Jamal-un-Nisa Bint, *The Qur'ān: Translation and Study*, Juz 1, 1984, 120pp.; Juz 2 and 3, 1987, 144pp.; Juz 4, 1992, 84pp., Ta-Ha Publishers, London.

RAHMAN, A.N.M. Wahidur, 'Modernists' Approach to the Qur'ān'. *Islam and the Modern Age* (New Delhi), 22, 2 (1991), 91-114.

RAHMAN, Fazlur, 'Translating the Qur'ān'. *Religion and Literature* (Notre Dame), 20, 1 (1988), 23-30.

———, *Major Themes of the Qur'ān*, Chicago, 1980.

RIPPIN, A., 'The Function of Asbāb al-Nuzūl in Qur'ānic Exegesis'. *Bulletin of the SOAS* (University of London), 51, Part 1 (1988), 1-20.

——— (ed.), *Approaches to the History of the Interpretation of the Qur'ān*. Clarendon Press, Oxford, 1988.

RUBIN, Uri, 'Exegesis and Ḥadīth: The Case of the Seven Mathānī'. In: G.R. Hawting and A.K.A. Shareef (eds.), *Approaches to the Qur'ān*. Routledge, London, 1993, 141-56.

———, 'The Shrouded Messenger – On the Interpretation of *al-Muzzammil* and *al-Muddaththir*'. *Jerusalem Studies in Arabic and Islam* (Jerusalem), 16 (1993), 96-107.

SADR, Al-Sayyid Muhamad Baqir AL-, 'The Holy Qur'ān and Laws of Historical Change'. *Al-Tawhid* (Tehran), 9, 4 (1992), 13-29; Part 2: 10, 2-3 (1993), 27-40.

SATTAR, Md. Abdus, 'Tafsīr Literature: An Evaluation'. *The Royal Asiatic Society of Bangladesh*, 31, 1 (1986), 129-36.

SAYYID, Allamah and TABATABA'I, M.H., *The Qur'ān in Islam: Its Impact and Influence on the Life of Muslims*. Kegan Paul, London, 1988.

Selections from the Qur'ān (Tr. P. Ghai). Independent Publishing Co. for Sterling Publishers India, London, 1992.

SHA'RAWI, Shaykh Muhammad Mitwalli AL-, *The Miracles of the Qur'ān* (Tr. M. Alserougii). Dar Al-Taqwa Ltd., London, 1990(?).

SMITH, Wilfred Cantwell, 'A Note on the Qur'ān from a Comparativist Perspective'. In: W.B. Hallaq and D.P. Little (eds.), *Islamic Studies Presented to Charles J. Adams*. Brill, Leiden, 1991, 183-92.

STANTON, H.U. Weitrecht, *The Teaching of the Qur'ān, with an account of its growth and subject index*. Darf, London, 1987.

STEWART, D.J., ' "Saj'" in the Qur'ān: Prosody and Structure'. *Journal of Arabic Literature* (Leiden), 21, 2 (1990), 101-39.

SURTY, Muhammad Ibrahim H.I., 'The Qur'ān in Islamic Scholarship: A Survey of *Tafsīr* Exegesis Literature in Arabic' (review article). *Muslim World Book Review* (Leicester), 7, 4 (Summer 1987), 51-65.

———, *A Course in the Science of Reciting the Qur'ān* (Includes two audio cassettes). The Islamic Foundation, Leicester, 1988.

———, *Towards Understanding Qur'ānic Arabic*. Qur'ānic Arabic Foundation, Birmingham, UK, 1993.

TABARI, A.J.M. ibn J. AL-, *Commentary on the Qur'ān*. Volume 1: Abridged English Translation (Tr. J. Cooper). Oxford University Press, 1986. Also published by The Islamic Texts Society, Cambridge, 1990.

TAYMIYAH, Imam Ibn, *An Introduction to the Exegesis of the Qur'ān* (Tr. Muhammad Abdul Haq Ansari). Islamic University of Imam Ibn Saud, Riyadh, 1989.

A Treasure of Qur'ānic Calligraphy. Hamdard Foundation Pakistan, Karachi, 1991.

USMANI, Muhammad Taqi, 'The History of The Preservation of the Qur'ān' (Tr. Muhammad Shameem). *Al-Balagh* (Karachi), 1, 4 (1990), 8-11.

USMANI, Shabbir Ahmad, *The Noble Qur'ān: Tafsīr-e-Usmani* (3 Vols.) (Tr. A. Ahmad). Aalamen Publications, Lahore, 1991.

WOOD, Kurt A., 'The Scientific Exegesis of the Qur'ān' (A Systematic Look). *MAAS Journal of Islamic Science* (Aligarh), 5, 2 (1989), 7-22.

Plate 1 *Jabal al-nūr* (Mount of Light) near Makka, with the cave of Hirā', where the Prophet received the first revelation. (*Sūra* 96: 1-5.) See p. 24.

Plate 2 Copy of the Holy Qur'ān, from the time of the Caliph 'Uthmān, kept in the Topkapi Museum, Istanbul. See p. 62.

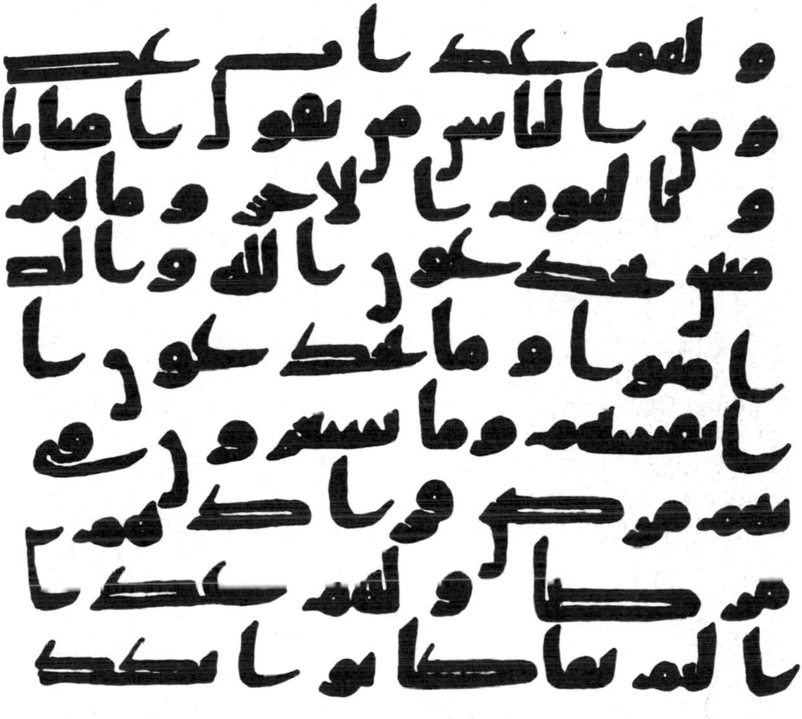

Plate 3 A page from the copy of the Holy Qur'ān, from the time of the Caliph 'Uthmān, kept in Tashkent. (*Sūra* 2:7-10; a part of the left margin has not been reproduced. Take your own Qur'ān and compare!) See p. 63.

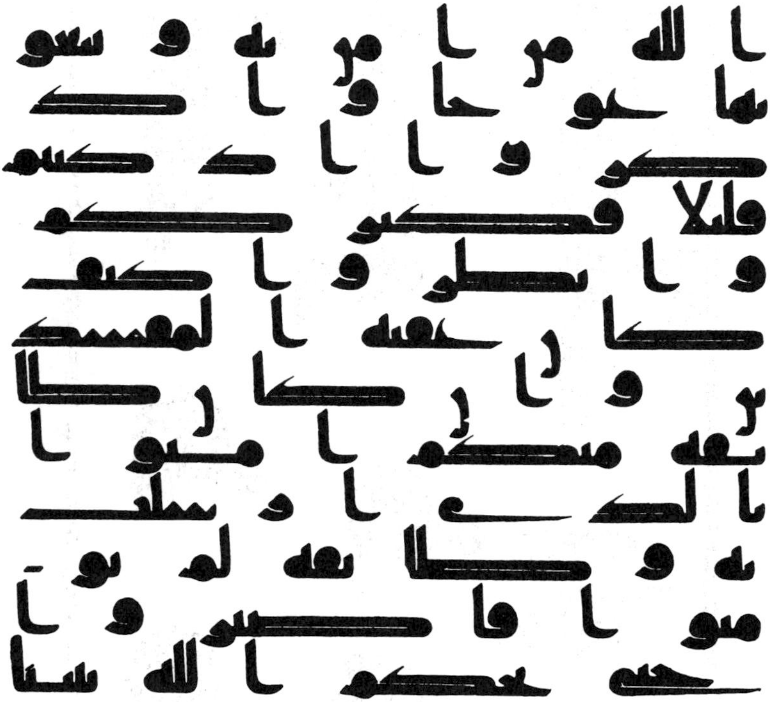

Plate 4 Another page from the copy of the Holy Qur'ān, from the time of the Caliph 'Uthmān, kept in Tashkent. (*Sūra* 7:86-87; take your own Qur'ān and compare!) See p. 63

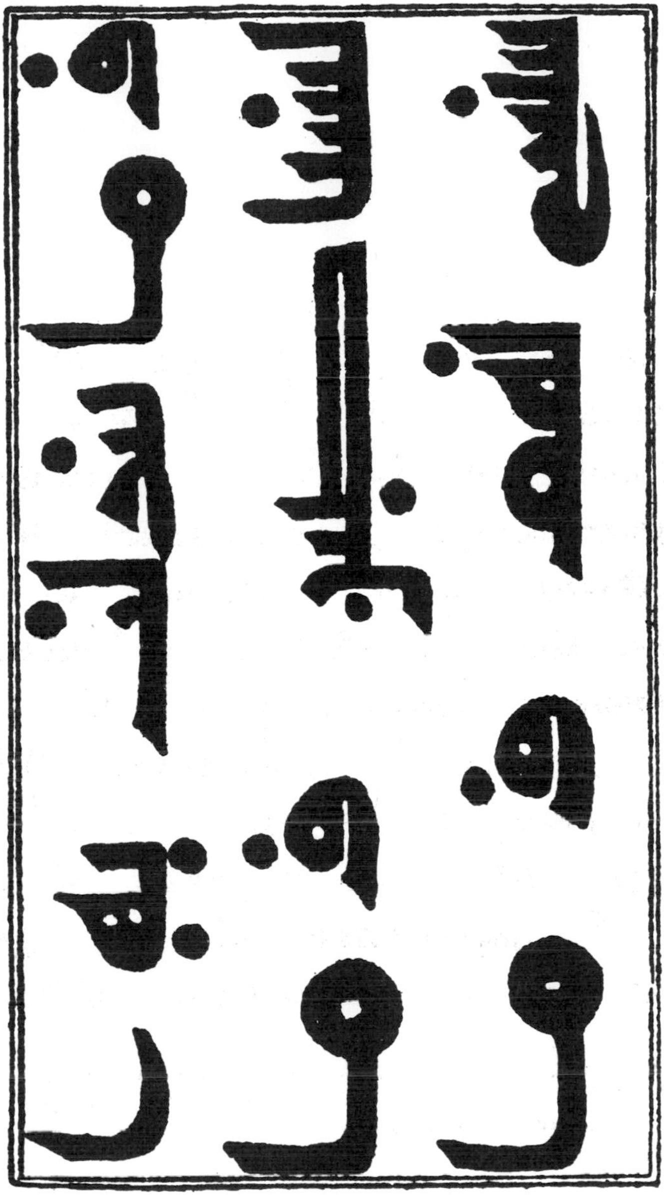

Plate 5 Part of a Qur'ān-manuscript in so-called Kufic writing, with *tashkīl* (vowel-marks) in the old style. (*Sūra* 26: 210-11.) See p. 58.

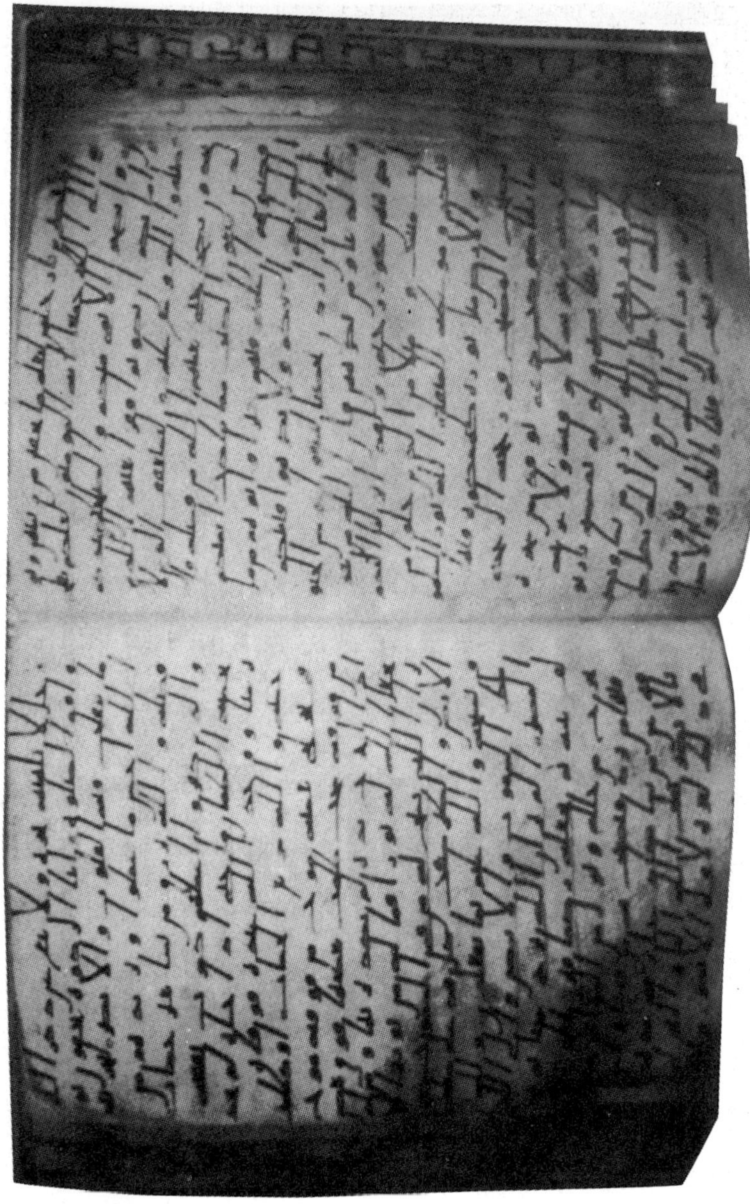

Plate 6 Two pages from an old manuscript of the Qur'ān, dated end of 2nd/8th century. It has a few vowel-marks and also indications of verse-endings (e.g. after verse 37) and end of *rukū'* (e.g. after verse 40). (*Sūra* 24: 32-36; 37-44.) See p. 61.

وأولئك هم المفلحون (4) إن الذين كفروا سواء
عليهم ءانذرتهم أم لم تنذرهم لا يومنون (5) ختم
الله على قلوبهم وعلى سمعهم وعلى أبصرهم
غشوة ولهم عذاب عظيم (6) ومن الناس من يقول
ءامنا بالله وباليوم الآخر وما هم بمومنين (7)
يخدعون الله والذين ءامنوا وما يخدعون إلا أنفسهم
وما يشعرون (8) في قلوبهم مرض فزادهم الله
مرضا ولهم عذاب أليم بما كانوا يكذبون
(9) وإذا قيل لهم لا تفسدوا في الأرض قالوا
إنما نحن مصلحون (10) ألا إنهم هم المفسدون ولكن
لا يشعرون (11) وإذا قيل لهم ءامنوا
كما ءامن الناس قالوا أنومن كما ءامن السفهاء
ألا إنهم هم السفهاء ولكن لا يعلمون (12) وإذا
لقوا الذين ءامنوا قالوا ءامنا وإذا خلوا إلى شيطينهم
قالوا إنا معكم إنما نحن مستهزءون (13) الله
يستهزئ بهم ويمدهم في طغينهم يعمهون (14)
أولئك الذين اشتروا الضللة بالهدى فما ربحت

Plate 7 A page from a printed Qur'ān from North Africa in *maghribī-script*. The text is vowelled according to the reading of Warsh. (*Sūra* 2: 4-15.) See p. 117.

أُوْلَٰٓئِكَ عَلَىٰ هُدًى مِّن رَّبِّهِمْۖ وَأُوْلَٰٓئِكَ هُمُ ٱلْمُفْلِحُونَ ﴿٥﴾
إِنَّ ٱلَّذِينَ كَفَرُواْ سَوَآءٌ عَلَيْهِمْ ءَأَنذَرْتَهُمْ أَمْ لَمْ تُنذِرْهُمْ
لَا يُؤْمِنُونَ ﴿٦﴾ خَتَمَ ٱللَّهُ عَلَىٰ قُلُوبِهِمْ وَعَلَىٰ سَمْعِهِمْۖ وَعَلَىٰٓ
أَبْصَٰرِهِمْ غِشَٰوَةٌۖ وَلَهُمْ عَذَابٌ عَظِيمٌ ﴿٧﴾ وَمِنَ ٱلنَّاسِ
مَن يَقُولُ ءَامَنَّا بِٱللَّهِ وَبِٱلْيَوْمِ ٱلْءَاخِرِ وَمَا هُم بِمُؤْمِنِينَ ﴿٨﴾
يُخَٰدِعُونَ ٱللَّهَ وَٱلَّذِينَ ءَامَنُواْ وَمَا يَخْدَعُونَ إِلَّآ أَنفُسَهُمْ
وَمَا يَشْعُرُونَ ﴿٩﴾ فِي قُلُوبِهِم مَّرَضٌ فَزَادَهُمُ ٱللَّهُ مَرَضًاۖ
وَلَهُمْ عَذَابٌ أَلِيمُۢ بِمَا كَانُواْ يَكْذِبُونَ ﴿١٠﴾ وَإِذَا قِيلَ لَهُمْ
لَا تُفْسِدُواْ فِي ٱلْأَرْضِ قَالُوٓاْ إِنَّمَا نَحْنُ مُصْلِحُونَ ﴿١١﴾
أَلَآ إِنَّهُمْ هُمُ ٱلْمُفْسِدُونَ وَلَٰكِن لَّا يَشْعُرُونَ ﴿١٢﴾ وَإِذَا
قِيلَ لَهُمْ ءَامِنُواْ كَمَآ ءَامَنَ ٱلنَّاسُ قَالُوٓاْ أَنُؤْمِنُ كَمَآ ءَامَنَ
ٱلسُّفَهَآءُۗ أَلَآ إِنَّهُمْ هُمُ ٱلسُّفَهَآءُ وَلَٰكِن لَّا يَعْلَمُونَ ﴿١٣﴾

Plate 8 A page from a printed Qur'ān from Jordan. The text is vowelled according to the reading of Ḥafṣ. (*Sūra* 2: 5-13.) See p. 117.